C000199722

PART 3
HANDBOOK

STEPHEN
BROOKHOUSE

RIBA ⊞ Publishing

© Stephen Brookhouse, 2007, 2011, 2014
Published by RIBA Publishing, 66 Portland Place, London, W1B 1NT

ISBN-978 1 85946 569 1

Stock Code 83007

Reprinted 2018

British Library Cataloguing in Publications Data
A catalogue record for this book is available from the British Library.

Commissioning Editor: Sarah Busby
Designed by Kneath Associates
Typeset by Academic + Technical, Bristol
Printed and bound by Charlesworth Press, Wakefield, WF2 9LP, UK

Image credits

10 Design Hong Kong	118, 153, 180
Make Architects Studio	Front cover
Stephen Brookhouse	18, 36, 174
Will Pryce	188, 204.

www.ribapublishing.com

PART 3
HANDBOOK
CONTENTS

FOREWORD

Part 3 is the culmination of an architect's formal education in Britain. It is the final gateway to being registered with the Architects Registration Board (ARB) and, in most cases, becoming a member of the Royal Institute of British Architects (RIBA). This is not to say that it is a prerequisite for producing great architecture; rather, it places on architects the standards and principles that define their relationships with society, clients, colleagues and those that commission and use their buildings. It provides the framework in which great architecture can germinate and grow, and it is what makes architects members of a recognised and respected profession.

As the third edition of this book shows, the Part 3 qualification bestows on architects the mantle of being acknowledged as experts with integrity, not just in the way they design and deliver great buildings, but also in the way they conduct themselves and lead others. Students must understand and embrace the codes of conduct issued by the ARB and RIBA, and indeed embrace the reasons behind them, as they provide a clear, ethical structure that validates calling oneself a British architect.

Most students assume that their undergraduate degree (Part 1) and their postgraduate qualifications (Part 2) provide most of the skills to practise as architects. This is not the case. Many students who successfully complete Part 3 realise that this course is the final part of a journey that brings with it a daunting adjustment to understanding the process of delivering what architects do – designing and helping to build our environment while dealing with regulation, contracts, disputes, practice issues, fees, business models and the plethora of matters that now confront architects daily as they help to make the world a better place. Part 3 is about ensuring competence in all these areas, guided by the principle of complete integrity.

Like most other professionals, architects are expected to exercise judgement – and this is something that constantly taxes students and qualified architects alike, even those with many years' experience. But this is really what Part 3 is about: measuring how you respond to technical and complex contractual or business issues, the way you exercise judgement in assessing options and selecting the way forward, and, most importantly, reflecting afterwards on whether these decisions have achieved the desired result. This excellent book shows the student the map, but without the light of judgement the path will remain obscure.

John Assael

Founder, Assael Architecture
RIBA Elected Member of Council
ARB Elected Board Member
Lecturer and External Examiner Part III

ACKNOWLEDGEMENTS

I would like to thank the students that I have worked with on the Part 3 examination over the past ten years whose experiences led to the idea for this book and whose feedback has informed this third edition; the Part 3 tutorial staff and professional examiners at the University of Westminster and the 'Part 3 community' of PSAs whose ideas and comments have informed its further development; and Sarah Busby at RIBA Enterprises without whose critical voice and support the project would not have happened. Special thanks should also go to 10 Design Architects and Master Planners, Hong Kong, Hawkins Brown Architects, London and Make Architects, London for their help with the photographs.

My thanks also to Alison Mackinder, Dyfed Griffiths and Samir Pandya for their assistance with the sample examination questions and Brian Henderson for the Mentor Guide.

Stephen Brookhouse

March 2014

INTRODUCTION

This book has been written primarily for students who are about to start the final part of their architectural education: the Part 3 examination. Unlike your earlier experiences of higher education, which comprised a set of stages along a path, Part 3 is the gateway to the profession. If you pass through that gateway and register as an architect, both the public and the architectural profession will expect a level of competency and skill in the conduct of your professional life that distinguishes you from other professionals in the construction industry. It is for this reason that Part 3 is taken so seriously by those involved in the delivery of Part 3 courses, the architectural practices that contribute to your professional development and the examiners that assess you.

For the Part 3 examination, what you learn in the workplace is more important than what you are taught in the classroom. Your main objective in Part 3 is to pass an examination and naturally what you are assessed on will act as a focus for your learning. This book concentrates on the separate elements that comprise the Part 3 examination, in the light of real experience. These elements, which all reflect your work-based learning, are: the Professional Experience and Development Record (known as the PEDR), your curriculum vitae and career appraisal, written examinations and/or coursework, the case study and the oral examination. The book is not a Part 3 'primer'; it does not contain the knowledge that you will need, except to show how it can be applied to best effect in the context of the elements that you are required to produce.

Even mature, postgraduate, part-time students, possibly with a Master's degree in addition to RIBA Parts 1 and 2, need guidance on how to make the most of work-based learning experience at this critical point in their professional development. The personal commitment and depth of part-time study that you must undertake in order to pass the examinations and assessments, both written and oral, is often not fully appreciated by students, employers and examiners. You will have to balance studying with your full-time professional work commitments and increasing professional responsibilities. However, the discipline needed to be successful in the Part 3 Examination mirrors that needed to be a successful architect.

One of the recurrent themes in the book is the necessity of mastering certain skills to equip yourself effectively for a career in architecture. Inevitably these skills include time management and presentation as well as the ability to work autonomously under pressure, all skills that you will have acquired to some extent in your career to date. One of the most sophisticated professional skills needed is that of reflection: the ability to challenge and review your experience and learn from it in an informed way. How you acquire these reflective skills and the importance of them permeates all parts of this book.

The context for Part 3, both politically and economically, has changed significantly since the first edition of this book was published. Despite the adverse effects of the economic recession on the construction industry, the architectural profession has risen to the challenge and deployed its many talents and skills to adapt to a fluid, more competitive professional environment. This book aims to guide Part 3 students through the last stage of formal professional education and help equip them for future – as yet unknown – challenges for the profession.

When you pass through the professional gateway it will be you and your fellow architects who will be shaping both the architectural profession and the built environment for the next 40 to 50 years.

How to use the book

The book uses the different components of the normal Part 3 submission as its structure. It takes you through each element, from the written examinations to the final interview, and gives guidance on how to satisfy the Part 3 Criteria (2010) and the appropriate standard of achievement. It does not duplicate technical, legal or managerial information that is available elsewhere unless it is helpful in illustrating or making a point. However, the appendices include sources that are referred to in the text and other useful information. Schools will have their own reading lists and preferred texts. It complements the information available on the PEDR website (www.pedr.co.uk), aiming to provide an appropriate framework within which you can place your knowledge and experience. To this effect it focuses on how to meet the assessment requirements – the 'outputs' – by guiding you through the process.

You do not need to read it from start to finish, but if you do you will get a comprehensive overview of what examiners are looking for in Part 3 candidates. You will make the best use of your time and avoid abortive work by reading the relevant chapter before you start that particular element of your Part 3 submission. Where the advice deviates from or contradicts the advice given by your school you will have to make up your own mind about which is most appropriate – but you should always follow the assessment requirements of your course. Over time, though, many course providers have elected to follow the advice in the book so any differences are likely to be relatively minor. However, the main objective is similar to that of Part 3: to provide best practice models as points of reference for your progress through this key experience in your professional development.

PREPARING FOR PART 3
CHAPTER 1

This chapter:

> *gives you an overview of the requirements for Part 3 and the professional and regulatory organisations that monitor and control it;*
> *explains the professional role of the architect in the construction industry, the rationale for the Part 3 examination and the organisations that control it;*
> *outlines the Criteria against which Part 3 students are judged;*
> *discusses in general terms the skills that students need to meet the standards set by the profession;*
> *explains your employer's role in supporting your personal development; and*
> *discusses how to choose the right Part 3 provider to suit your individual strengths.*

The professional architect

Part 3 is the culmination of a long period of architectural education, a process that was established many years ago: a three-year degree leading to Part 1, a year of professional experience (Stage 1), and a further two years of postgraduate study leading to a further academic award – Part 2.[1] However, many students who pass Part 2 decide not to continue with Part 3 without necessarily leaving the business of architecture. For example, it is possible to go on to senior positions in large practices or teach in schools of architecture without the Part 3 examination under your belt. In both situations you can influence and shape the architectural education and professional development of future architectural professionals. In the UK, although the title of 'architect' is protected, the role is not. In short, anyone can practise architecture, but only if you have passed Part 3 and are registered with the ARB can you call yourself an architect. This begs the question, 'Why bother with Part 3?' Having got this far you are likely to have your own view, but it is a good starting point for introducing the concept of what it means to be a professional architect.

If you are reading this book, you are likely to be on the threshold of undertaking the Part 3 examination. By now you will have considerable knowledge of design and construction and will understand that the architect is a member of a multidisciplinary professional team. The process of designing and constructing buildings will have been revealed as requiring the implementation and coordination of a complex set of activities carried out by many different people. Each project is characterised by uncertainty, risk and a certain fluidity. This coming together of diverse groups for a single purpose has been described as a 'temporary multi-organisation'.[2] However, the physical results are far from temporary, remaining in place for a considerable time, and mistakes can be costly to both owners and occupiers and sometimes their architects.

Architects are a key, if sometimes relatively small (at least in terms of numbers of people), part of the construction industry. The industry, in turn, comprises approximately ten per cent of our economy, and UK expertise in design and construction contributes significantly to exports. It is a global industry with international contractors, designers and suppliers. The industry, though, is characterised by fragmentation and, not surprisingly, few commentators can agree on its boundaries. There are also several different professions involved in delivering buildings and the relationships between these different parties are not always clear. The industry is also characterised by spectacular multi-million pound disputes arising out of this uncertainty and complexity. Within this fluid, project-led environment it is essential to know what each key professional does and the boundaries of their respective knowledge and skills.

Professions have been defined as having four distinct defining characteristics. They must:

> own a distinct body of knowledge;
> erect barriers to entry to maintain standards;
> serve the public interest; and
> enjoy mutual recognition from other professions.[3]

Architects own a clear body or 'silo' of knowledge and competence that is distinct from the other 'silos of knowledge' held by other members of the design and construction team, such as quantity surveyors or structural engineers. By the time you reach Part 3 that knowledge will already be both wide and deep. Now you will be expected to acquire new knowledge as well as continue to broaden and deepen existing competencies. The professional bodies, architectural practice and the schools of architecture all contribute to this body of knowledge, which is expressed in a set of Professional Criteria which effectively sets the reasonable boundaries for this professional knowledge and competence. These Professional Criteria will be discussed in more detail later.

How to demonstrate your competence and the standards to be met are set by the profession and – to an extent – the public and maintained by the professional institutions. In reference to our definition of a profession, this is the 'barrier to entry', the quality control measure imposed by professions requiring a mix of recognised educational qualifications and relevant professional experience. The two overriding objectives in setting these barriers are, first, to protect the public and, second, to maintain the reputation of the profession. For the architectural profession in the UK, the Part 3 examination functions as the final barrier, the last point of control.

Mutual recognition by other professionals is important, especially in the complex environment of design and construction. A profession that is not recognised by other professions has little or no effective status. The professional bodies therefore work hard to be members of a network of similar professions. Professional bodies seek wider recognition to reinforce their position. Traditionally, the royal charter that gives members 'chartered' status is the highest form of accolade and ensures recognition by other chartered professions. Uniquely in the construction industry, architects have their own statutory control as well as professional membership. In other words, two bodies control the profession: the Architects Registration Board (ARB) – the statutory authority – and the Royal Institute of British Architects (RIBA) – the professional internship body.

Linked with this idea of 'public protection' is the public interest: the professions place the public good above financial reward. This is typically expressed generally as maintaining impartiality and is, in effect, a trade-off for public recognition. In particular this principle is expanded upon and stated publicly in a set of professional standards and ethical codes of practice which exceed normal commercial standards of 'fair delivery'.

This aspect of the profession of architecture (and the professions in general) has changed significantly in recent years in the eyes of the public, with the public demanding more of them and putting them under increased scrutiny with allegations of restrictive practices that are neither competitive nor transparent. Despite these concerns the traditional professions continue to survive but their status has diminished. For example, the status of the parish priest as a figure of moral authority is diminished, the local doctor has his or her judgement questioned, accountants and lawyers continue to be embroiled in international criminal proceedings following spectacular company failures. Nonetheless, in a fast-changing and demanding world, special knowledge and expertise is at a premium, and the professions continue to be the best model for developing a secure knowledge base.

From these characteristics you will see that some 'professions' fail the tests of barriers to entry, mutual recognition and public interest. Hairdressers and footballers, for example, who are sometimes described as professionals, do not make it because they do not serve the 'public interest'. Efforts to professionalise traffic wardens and cleaners through training and qualifications are unlikely to bring them the same level of professional recognition as architects and engineers.

Part 3 has been developed within the professional context of architectural practice. It will continue to develop as the demands on the profession change. At present it is set within a secure recognised framework, the Professional Criteria held in common by the RIBA and the ARB.

The ARB and the RIBA

The Architects Registration Board (ARB) and the Royal Institute of British Architects (RIBA) are the two controlling bodies affecting architectural education in general and at Part 3 in particular. Part 3 is especially important as it is the gateway to professional practice and, as such, is distinct from the earlier steps in your education. The following summaries will give you a clear idea of how each organisation came into existence, where they obtain their powers, what or who controls them and their key functions.

THE ARB

The ARB is a statutory body established by Parliament in 1997 to regulate the architects' profession in the UK.[4] It draws its powers from the Architects Act 1997 and has five key functions:

1. Prescribing – or 'recognising' the qualifications needed to become an architect.
2. Keeping the UK Register of Architects.
3. Ensuring that architects meet the standards for conduct and practice.
4. Investigating complaints about an architect's conduct or competence.
5. Making sure that only people on the register offer their services as an architect.[5]

As a statutory body the ARB is also the vehicle for enacting any relevant European legislation. The ARB is the UK's designated competent authority for architects under the Mutual Recognition of Professional Qualifications Directive [2005/36/EC] (as amended in 2013 by 2013/55/EU), which facilitates the recognition of qualifications for architects arising from the Directive. It also examines professionals from outside the EU to ensure that they meet the published General Criteria.[6]

As the 'competent authority' the ARB now effectively controls the gateway to professional registration and the recognition of UK Part 3 qualifications across the other EU states. Because the free movement of labour is one of the basic principles of the EU – and the professions by their nature erect barriers to entry – EU states work together to try and ensure that the standards and competence of comparable professions are recognised across the EU.

In order to strengthen mutual recognition of the professions amongst EU states the 2005 Directive has been subject to lengthy and thorough review. The result is that an amended Directive (2013/55/EU) was agreed and published in 2013.

The UK, guided by the ARB, entered a period of consultation in early 2014 in order to agree how the European Directive will be implemented. It should be noted that the Directive does not apply just to architects but to all major professions including doctors, solicitors, veterinary surgeons, etc. (Sections 46 and 47 of the Directive are the ones relevant to the training of architects.)

Because of its far-reaching nature the Directive is not set to be in force until 2018 and therefore does not affect you. However, this brief survey also shows how European legislation (in this case a European Directive) 'cascades' down into the UK legislation and practice.

The objectives of this statutory body broadly align with the characteristics of a profession by setting the barriers for entry and policing public interest issues by disciplining registered architects who do not meet the standards laid down in its Code of Conduct and Standards (2010). In addition, it has the further role of protecting the title 'architect' by prosecuting individuals or organisations that pass themselves off as such. This is seen as another way of protecting the public interest. The public interest mission is further reinforced by the composition of the ARB's 15-member controlling Board, where elected architects are in the minority and 'lay' members prevail. The eight lay members are appointed by the Privy Council[7] 'to represent the interests of users of architectural services and the general public'.[8] The seven architect members are elected by the profession itself. In 2014 the chair had a background in public sector procurement and the vice-chair was an architect. Previous chairs have included a retired judge.

The ARB is a stripped down version of an earlier body, ARCUK (the Architects Registration Council of the United Kingdom),[9] which had around 70 Council Members with very few non-architect members. It also had limited disciplinary powers that did not deal with issues of competency. The rationale for the change was the widespread pressure to modernise the structure of regulation for architects against the general background of the public's desire to make all the professions more openly accountable.

The ARB is led by its Registrar who heads up a small staff, which is divided into three main teams: Registration, Regulation and Qualifications. Disciplinary matters are handled by the Professional Conduct Committee (PCC) made up of publicly appointed lay members and publicly appointed architect members.

THE RIBA

The RIBA's remit is wider than the ARB's: to promote architecture as well as uphold the standards of the profession. Its vision is to be a 'champion for architecture and for a better environment'.[10] It is a membership organisation (with approximately 30,000 members) and was granted its first Royal Charter in 1837.[11] There are also byelaws that provide the RIBA's operational framework. These are approved by the Privy Council.

The RIBA sets out its mission as follows:

> The RIBA champions better buildings, communities and the environment through architecture and our members. We provide the standards, training, support and recognition that put our members – in the UK and overseas – at the peak of their profession.
>
> With Government we work to improve the design quality of public buildings, new houses and new communities.[12]

As you would expect, it has barriers to entry (you cannot join as a 'chartered member' unless you have completed Parts 1, 2 and 3). It has a Code of Conduct, disciplining members that fail to meet its standards, has a key role in architectural education and also acts as a resource for members in practice. In terms of our key characteristics of a profession, it is prominent through its role in education and practice, in defining and maintaining the architectural 'silo of knowledge'. Its Council, the large majority of whom are chartered architects (generally elected by other members), controls the RIBA and is responsible for its conduct and development. As such and in contrast to the ARB, there is no direct public representation.

The RIBA has two main parts: RIBA Council and the RIBA Board.

> RIBA Council is the 'charter body' and is ultimately responsible for the conduct and development of the institute. It comprises 60 members, the large majority of whom are chartered architects.
>
> The Council passes down detailed responsibility and technical focus to the RIBA Board and executive.

The RIBA Board is the group board, responsible for directing the overall business of the RIBA. It operates under the overall authority and policy of the elected Council.[13]

The RIBA is led by a Chief Executive and has a number of departments in London and a presence in the regions and nations of the UK and has a staff of around 200. For example RIBA Professional Services has four departments: Education, Research and Development, Practice and Membership. The RIBA also relies on its membership to contribute to the running of the institute through a series of committees, with particular responsibilities: for example Education.

REVIEWING THE PROFESSION

The two organisations are very different in their objectives and character. However, some of their roles, including education and discipline, overlap. This sometimes leads to friction. The issue of whether the public or the profession wanted a statutory registration body in addition to the RIBA was reviewed in the early 1990s as part of a general government review of statutory regulation and culminated in the Warne Report of 1993, which recommended deregulation.[14] However the RIBA and its members lobbied hard for continuing registration. Hence the creation of the ARB.

During the early 2000s the RIBA began to take the view that the ARB was exceeding the powers granted in the 1997 Act and lobbied government, unsuccessfully, for a review. In 2010, following the election of the Coalition Government, the ARB was reviewed together with all 'quangos'[15] as part of a wider review of the government's mission and involvement. This was part of a well-publicised drive to cut 'red tape' and government bureaucracy in order to help reduce the economy's structural deficit. This time the RIBA changed its position and lobbied for the dismantling of the ARB and the transfer of its main functions to the RIBA. The ARB survived the review intact. The main reason given by the government was that the ARB had a technical function that could not be provided satisfactorily by any other body. Its independent regulatory function is also seen as a model for other professions and to move these functions to the professional membership body, the RIBA, was seen as contrary to the general trend in society of the independent review of professions and the wider representation of consumers in the conduct of professionals.

In most other EU states, by contrast, only one body, the professional members' organisation, controls entry to the profession and administers the Architects' Directive. In the UK you have to pay a registration fee to the ARB to call yourself an architect and have the choice of paying, in addition, a membership fee to the RIBA to call yourself a chartered architect. The majority of the profession follow the latter route.

Fortunately both organisations agree on the standards for entry to the profession and the knowledge, skills and competencies required for practice. These are set out in the Professional Criteria for Part 3 that are held 'in common' by the RIBA and the ARB.

Both organisations exert significant control over the Part 3 examination. The ARB 'prescribes' qualifications through a paper-based exercise and the RIBA 'validates' courses and qualifications through its four-year cycle of inspections and intermediate visits. Each organisation requires schools of architecture[16] to map the delivery and assessment of the Part 3 course against the agreed Professional Criteria.

DISCIPLINARY MATTERS

Both the ARB and the RIBA take disciplinary matters very seriously, as you would expect given that this is central to the idea of the 'public interest'.

In order to demonstrate that the 'public interest' is maintained – and in the case of the ARB – that the consumer of architectural services is protected – it is essential that both bodies effectively police the minimum standards of competence and conduct. These are set out in the RIBA Code of Conduct (2009) and the ARB's Code of Conduct (2010).

It will come as no surprise that you must be familiar with both codes as they set the minimum acceptance standards for you as an architect in practice as employee, employer and (especially) as a sole practitioner.

The Architects Act 1997 sets out the disciplinary powers of the ARB. The ARB is obliged, as a consumer-facing organisation, to take each complaint seriously. Complainants can download a complaint form from the ARB website and then answer a short questionnaire. Not all complaints are valid but nevertheless all have to be considered. It is a transparent process and both the complainant and the architect concerned are circulated with each other's correspondence, allegations and responses. Both parties are encouraged to mediate the problem but some complaints go to the heart of professional conduct and may warrant prosecution under the 1997 Act. The decision to pass a case to a disciplinary tribunal is taken initially by the ARB's Investigation Panel (IP), which effectively acts as a filter for complaints. This committee's representation mirrors that of the Board with a majority of lay members. The three architect members give technical and contextual advice. The IP does not have any disciplinary powers but may give limited advice and issue a caution. The process is private and confidential and the IP does not publish its decisions. However if the IP considers that there is a 'case to answer' it notifies the complainant and the architect and passes the casework to the Registrar. It is then for the ARB's solicitor to make a case for prosecution under the Architects Act 1997. The ARB can only prosecute on two grounds: i) serious professional incompetence and ii) unacceptable professional conduct. The Code and Standards (2010) act as guidelines – and inevitably overlap in content. The ARB's PCC acts as an independent tribunal – the ARB makes its case, and the architect gives a response (similar to a defence) and the PCC arrives at an independent decision, which either party may appeal to the High Court.[17] At no time is the tribunal acting for the ARB. Each tribunal is chaired by a solicitor who sits with one lay member and one architect. The PCC can issue a very limited number of penalties, from a reprimand to removal from the register: 'erasure'. (The range of penalties is published on the ARB website.) The hearings are held in public and are reported in the press if the matter is of public interest. The ARB also publishes the decisions on its website. These are worth reading to get a flavour of the issues that result in prosecution. From around 500 initial complaints made annually by the public about 12 are considered serious enough to reach a tribunal.

It should be emphasised that the ARB cannot resolve disputes. It will only act if it considers that there is a case to answer for unacceptable professional conduct or serious professional incompetence. Most cases relate to conduct but occasionally the architect's competence is questioned. The ARB has no power to become involved in the disputes nor can it award compensation.

The majority of complaints received by the ARB fall into the following categories:

1. Failure to provide a clear written contract for professional services.
2. Failure to confirm the price to be charged for services.
3. Matters relating to planning applications.
4. Inadequate budget and cost advice.
5. Failure to manage tendering procedures.
6. Contract administration.
7. Technical matters relating to design and production information.

By far, the most common complaint is the architect's failure to manage client expectations by failing to provide a clear and written contract for professional services. The ARB's requirement to confirm your contract in writing is a good example of how the professions set standards that exceed normal commercial and legal practice where an oral contract is considered acceptable.

The RIBA has recently reviewed its disciplinary procedures. Before the review disciplinary proceedings were held 'in camera' by its Hearings Panel. The Panel was made up of chartered members who were appointed in a less than transparent way to make decisions about other chartered members based on complaints brought by the public which were rarely published. The new process is administered by the Professional Standards section of the Practice Department and its Professional Services Board. The emphasis, understandably, is on architectural practice and the relationship between client and architect, a reflection of the membership it represents and their source of income.

Although there are many similarities between the RIBA and ARB processes, the RIBA takes as its starting point that complaints generally arise because of a dispute between clients and their architects. As a first step it encourages early resolution of disputes. Complainants and architects are encouraged to mediate and to this effect the RIBA offers a free telephone consultation with a specialist consultant. If this fails complainants may lodge a formal complaint. Cases are first assessed by an appraisal team made up of two chartered members and one non-member. The complaint may then be passed to a Hearings Panel made up of three non-members with at least one RIBA Chartered member as a non-voting expert adviser. The RIBA does not, unlike the ARB, appoint a solicitor to make its case to a tribunal.

The Panel considers the complaint in relation to the relevant Byelaws. The allegations are then considered in relation to its own Code of Professional Conduct or whether the architect:

> *behaved in a manner that is considered to be unacceptable in a professional person.*[18]

In theory this last statement gives the complainant and the Panel a much wider remit. It also aligns with one of the concepts referred to earlier that underpins professionalism – the mutual recognition and respect of other professionals. The potential grounds for a complaint, therefore, go far wider than the RIBA's own Code of Conduct or the ARB's Code and Standards. In practice, it would be very difficult to prove a case on this basis alone.

Because the RIBA's procedures are concerned with disciplining its members, rather than conducting a prosecution under the Architect's Act, the sanctions available are limited to a private or public reprimand, suspension or exclusion. The RIBA cannot fine members nor can it award compensation or damages. Although the two processes are independent of each other in practice the process can be duplicated and complainants generally lodge a complaint with the ARB and RIBA simultaneously. When a member is sanctioned by the ARB, the RIBA will also consider referring the member to the Hearings Panel. It is also very unlikely that the RIBA and ARB will come to different decisions, although in theory they may as each organisation has different objectives and powers. But it is questionable whether the additional expense and time spent in effect duplicating disciplinary processes serve the best interests of the public or the profession.[19]

It is worth remembering these disciplinary functions. The standards that the ARB and RIBA set in their Codes are the standards that you will be agreeing to meet when you pass Part 3 and enter the profession. They are highly valued by the public and the profession. Architects who transgress not only risk personal sanction but also threaten the wider perception of the profession, hence the need to monitor professional behaviour. Interestingly, the Government's Attorney General has relatively recently emphasised the role and importance of the professions themselves, rather than the courts, in regulating and disciplining their members.[20]

The most important point to remember is that as the professions set high entry barriers and rely on the trust and respect of the public, very high standards of conduct – which exceed normal commercial standards of behaviour – are required to retain this relatively privileged position.

The Part 3 Professional Criteria 2010

You will see that the Professional Criteria for Part 3 are important because they crystallise the key knowledge, skills and competence that characterise architects as a separate and distinct profession in the construction industry. They also reflect the public interest in the competence to practise. The full Professional Criteria for Part 3 can be referred to in Appendix 1 and you should familiarise yourself with them. Although each Part 3 provider is required to meet the Professional Criteria this is not always made explicit in their course documents.

The Criteria are framed in five key areas:

PC1 Professionalism
PC2 Clients, users and delivery of services
PC3 Legal framework and processes
PC4 Practice and management
PC5 Building procurement

The Criteria set out the minimum levels of knowledge, understanding and ability that students must acquire. They represent a considered but broad view of what an architect should be able to do without either endangering the trust that the public in general and clients in particular have in them or undermining the professional standing of the profession as a whole. They provide a snapshot of the profession as viewed by members of the profession, the ARB and everyone else who was consulted, including co-professionals at the time the Part 3 Professional Criteria were last reviewed and published in 2010. Having been arrived at by consensus the Professional Criteria are inevitably broad and inclusive. The relevance for you as you start Part 3 is that there will be many areas to which you have not been exposed in your current professional

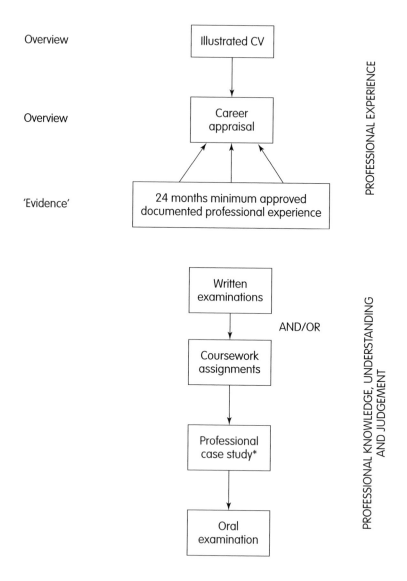

Overview — Illustrated CV

Overview — Career appraisal

'Evidence' — 24 months minimum approved documented professional experience

PROFESSIONAL EXPERIENCE

Written examinations

AND/OR

Coursework assignments

Professional case study*

Oral examination

PROFESSIONAL KNOWLEDGE, UNDERSTANDING AND JUDGEMENT

*Note: A small minority of schools of architecture do not require a case study.

FIGURE 1.1 The components of the Part 3 Examination

experience and where you do not have adequate knowledge. At worst, some of the Professional Criteria will appear to be irrelevant to current architectural practice as you perceive it. However, the qualification allows you to practise *as an individual* using the protected title – what professional examiners refer to as the 'brass plaque test'. There is, especially at this stage in your career, an unavoidable tension or mismatch between your specific experience and the wider requirements for registration.

The way you demonstrate that you meet the Professional Criteria is through submission of a number of written components and an oral examination carried out by two Professional Examiners. It includes (Figure 1.1):

> a curriculum vitae;
> a career evaluation;
> a minimum of 24 months of recorded professional experience using the professional experience and development record (PEDR);
> written examinations;
> coursework;
> a case study.

The four terms used in the Professional Criteria – 'knowledge, understanding, ability and skills' – are borrowed from the world of education; 'knowledge' picks up on the 'silos of knowledge' discussed above. The distinction between 'knowledge' and 'understanding' is harder to define, although 'understanding' can be seen as 'transformative' – providing insight or doing something with the knowledge you have gained. 'Ability' can be seen as being the *practical* application of knowledge, demonstrating professional competence. Professionals also demonstrate good judgement in their decision-making and conduct and it is this last quality, judgement, that Professional Examiners are looking for in particular in your written work and in the oral examination.

Skills

Another way of approaching the practical aspects of your professional competence is to think about developing your relevant skills and the Criteria, rightly, reflect the importance of professional skills. During your academic career and through your professional experience and development you have acquired particular skills. For example, the ability to design and to apply computer skills spring readily to mind, along with visual and written presentation skills. The skills needed for Part 3 build on these existing skills but require you to demonstrate them at a more advanced level appropriate for a professional qualification, which is generally equivalent to Master's degree level. A well-written Part 3 course handbook will make these skills explicit. They may include the following:

1. *Group working*: as both a leader and a member in the workplace; delegating and managing tasks and handling conflict.
2. *Autonomy*: working with the minimum of guidance.
3. *Resourcing*: using technical, legal and commercial sources of information.
4. *Management and information*: managing time and completing tasks with the minimum of guidance.
5. *Problem-solving*: using creative and numeracy skills to evaluate issues.
6. *Communication*: engaging competently in professional reporting both verbally and in writing. (Examples include preparing a brief or design statement and making a presentation.)
7. *Reflective practice*: demonstrating continuous personal professional development through informed, structured self-evaluation.[21]

You will probably be familiar with most of these. You will see that at Part 3 level these are acquired on the course and in the workplace and, unlike undergraduate programmes, you are expected to develop these mostly autonomously. Skills 2, 3, 4, 5 and 7 all share the characteristic of independent competence which relates directly to the ARB and RIBA concept of the independent practitioner – the 'brass plaque test'. Schools of architecture try to develop reflective practice in their professional and managerial studies at Part 1 and Part 2 levels but it is especially important at Part 3. It is worth considering it in more detail as it is a thread that runs through every element of your academic portfolio.

Reflective practice: learning from experience and professional development

Reflective skills are essential to your professional development. Architectural practice is not simply a matter of applying and repeating general principles according to a set of rules. Just because you have always done something in a certain way, it does not follow that you should carry on doing it that way. 'Reflection' as a term is slightly misleading. It does not mean the kind of reflection you see in a mirror, which is an exact replica of the object. Rather, it is reflection in the sense of considering a matter meditatively. Reflection in professional practice is thinking about something in a structured way to see how it could have been done better.

The role of a theory or model is sometimes to change 'what is' to 'what might be'. In the context of architectural practice, we constantly refer to 'best practice models'. It might be the Code of Conduct that informs our professionalism, or a set of regulations or guidelines such as the CDM Regulations that informs your approach to health and safety or a set of standard tendering procedures that ensure fair play in contracting. Whatever it is, the model makes you aware that there is a problem and helps you articulate it and generate a solution. You need to *know* and *understand* the professional points of reference in order to reshape a problem, arrive at a conclusion and be *able* to implement it *competently*. You can see that this process of reflection is at the heart of professionalism – an essential professional skill. In your written work and at your professional interview/oral examination you should show that you have:

1. *identified* a problem
2. *examined* it using profession points of reference
3. *reached* a conclusion
4. *considered* how it may inform and improve future practice.

To do so shows an ability to reflect on a problem and should win you positive marks.

You should note that the process of reflection is more than self-referential navel-gazing. It requires an informed view that compares current experience with professional standards of behaviour and the current professional knowledge base. It also implies that you should never take anything at face value. This skill is very different from the task-orientated technical skills that are also highly valued in architectural practice. Examiners will be looking for evidence of reflective practice in your written work and in the oral examination. It is a theme that runs throughout assessment at Part 3.

The role of practice in preparing for Part 3

Part 3 is a three-way partnership between you, your practice and your school of architecture. The role of practice in architectural education is a topic regularly debated by the RIBA, the schools and architectural practices. The role of practice in Part 3 is pivotal because, unlike Parts 1 and 2, Part 3 is essentially work-based. The workplace is your key learning resource, without which Part 3 would be impossible to pass. This is echoed by the RIBA Regulations for Part 3 and the ARB's Rules (Rule 13b), which require you to be working under the direct supervision of a registered architect or a similarly qualified member of an appropriate professional body involved in the procurement, design and management of the built environment. Ideally, your practical experience should be in a design environment, but both the RIBA and the ARB recognise the value of working with other members of the design and construction team.

Your office has three key functions that affect your professional development. The first is to provide you with a mentor to discuss and develop the depth and breadth of your experience, to facilitate reflection and to use the quarterly PEDR sheets as a way of recording your development in the context of the Part 3 Criteria. The second is to allow you to work on (or, exceptionally, 'shadow') a project that follows the RIBA Plan of Work and is a suitable subject for a case study. The third is a general one: to provide a supportive environment that enables you to develop your knowledge and experience and to set an example of professional competence for you to follow. The absence of any of these functions will affect your progress in Part 3.

Your mentor is there not only to offer support but also to discuss 'best practice' – enormously helpful in your efforts to reflect on practice, a process identified above as essential to your professional development. The choice of case study is equally important and is considered in detail later in this book. The role of the PEDR and guidance on its use is given on the PEDR website and you should make every effort to use it as a vehicle for your professional development in the workplace.

Architectural practices are busy places and the office's main mission will be to provide a service to its clients. Supporting your development has a direct beneficial effect on your contribution as an employee and project team member. Architects in the office will also be committed to CPD and some work-based learning. However, in a pressured environment it is sometimes difficult to make the time to support Part 3 students. You will need to develop good time management, negotiation and communication skills as well as an ability to work autonomously in order to achieve your personal goal of completing Part 3.

Choosing a Part 3 provider

Every school of architecture or provider that offers Part 3 has to assess students against the Criteria and to a recognised standard, and not all schools offer Part 3. For example, the RIBA North-West Region provides Part 3 for the Liverpool and Manchester schools of architecture. APEAS is solely an examining body created by the Scottish schools of architecture and carries out the Part 3 examination on their behalf. Part 3 courses are delivered in a variety of ways and, within certain limits, will have their own preferred methods of assessment. Some offer a series of short courses, some deliver the course in a more structured way. They should all have some independent quality assurance and periodic review system that monitors the course content, the delivery and the resources allocated to deliver and assess the course effectively. When it comes to assessment, most schools use time-limited written examinations, sometimes in the workplace, and ask you to write a case study. A few schools may use continuous assessment for the written part of the academic submission.

Your choice of provider may be influenced by the method of assessment but convenience, reputation and the level of academic support should also be factors that you take into consideration. Anecdotal evidence from recent Part 3 students is usually very unreliable when it comes to their experience in the oral examination but it is worth talking to colleagues in your office and elsewhere about their experiences of the course content and delivery. For a full list of Part 3 providers, please see Appendix 3.

The cost of the course may also be a determining factor. In comparing costs, you should start by looking at your own level of knowledge and experience. Some courses are 'refresher' courses which in effect help you to refine skills you already have in preparation for the examination. At the other end of the spectrum, there are courses that deliver substantial lecture series and provide significant support in the preparation of your case study and your professional development in general. You should also realise that the cost is only a small part of the total resource required to pass Part 3 in terms of the time you give to it and the support you receive (possibly also financial) from your office.

Wherever possible you should be looking for the 'added value' that a Part 3 provider brings to the preparation for the written examinations and/or coursework, your case study and supporting your professional redevelopment. Websites are not always helpful here so do what you would do in the office: ask colleagues and call the provider and talk to the course director. Look at the course team's curricula vitae (which should be available on the website) and for any particular expertise or achievements as well as publications.

PROFESSIONAL DEVELOPMENT: LEARNING FROM EXPERIENCE IN THE WORKPLACE AND THE PEDR
CHAPTER 2

This chapter:

> *will assist you in preparing your CV, Professional Education and Development Record (PEDR) and career appraisal to pass the professional development element of the Part 3 submission;*
> *discusses how to record your experience effectively and accurately, the different parts of the professional development element and their role in the examination; and*
> *looks at how examiners review your experience and how this, in turn, forms the basis for some of the questioning you will face at the oral examination.*

'Experience is the museum of mistakes' [German proverb]

This chapter does not intend to repeat advice already available online on the RIBA's website[1] for recording your work-based experience, which you are advised to consult in conjunction with the advice given here.

It is widely recognised that academic study is not enough to achieve the levels of knowledge and competence to practice as an architect. Your work-based learning is a key element of your professional development.

At a simple level there is a basic requirement for 24 months of practical experience to be gained in a way approved by the RIBA and ARB and recorded consistently. Therefore your 24 months of experience is the gateway to the examination – in other words you cannot take oral examination without reaching this milestone.

In principle, it is not the quality of your experience that is being assessed – only the number of months (24). In practice, because your experience is so important as a way of gaining knowledge and understanding, the professional examiners will want to see how your experience has contributed to your holistic professional development and therefore how you meet the Professional Criteria.

It must be stressed at this point that you need not have experienced directly every aspect of architectural practice – this is probably impossible. Therefore examiners are assessing your knowledge and experience against the Professional Criteria at the point that the profession and the public expect as a reasonable level of competence – ideally gained within 24 months but certainly not the standard you will achieve after 24 years! Your record of experience – as evidence of your practical training – is only one element of the Part 3 examination and will be read in conjunction with your coursework, written examinations, case study and your performance in the oral examination to assess whether or not you meet the Professional Criteria at the required level of competence to practise as an architect.

Some myths

1. 'You require direct work experience of all RIBA Work Stages' [Not true]
   The requirement is to meet the Professional Criteria at the required level. This includes knowledge and understanding of project delivery – and many other subject areas. The principle that you are meeting the Professional Criteria rather than RIBA Work Stages is complicated by the format of the RIBA PEDR which concentrates on – although not exclusively – the Work Stages. This is because the PEDR is only part of the evidence you provide at Part 3 and is not conclusive evidence of meeting all the Professional Criteria.

2. 'You must have direct experience of contract administration' [Not True]
   This myth is perpetuated, in part, by the format of PEDR. Thankfully the new RIBA Plan of Work acknowledges the diversity and complexity of architectural practice in the 21st century.
   There is a very sound argument that in order to maintain the professional principle of 'Public Protection' you must know and understand the role the architect plays as the client's agent and contract administrator resolving contractor claims – particularly in smaller contracts where the client is likely to be a domestic consumer and end-user. Also, the significant majority of architectural practices work for end-user clients.
   The problem faced by Part 3 providers is that the administration of traditional contractor contracts is complex and fluid – making it difficult to teach comprehensively based on theory alone. However it is very difficult to gain this experience directly – especially when correct architectural practice is so diverse. Also, direct experience of contract administration alone does not guarantee knowledge of best practice provided by your lectures and key reference texts to contribute to your competence in this area.

Part 3 providers and examiners recognise this as a challenge. Part 3 providers will deliver the basic building blocks that allow you to study independently basic contractual procedures and 'best practice' models and Part 3 examiners will probe this area of knowledge as a way of assessing your competence. For this reason: 'Experience (even if you have it) is not enough'.

The RIBA and ARB set out the minimum requirements for your work experience. These are available on the RIBA website (www.pedr.co.uk) and on the ARB website (www.arb.org.uk). You should refer to these requirements and have a working knowledge of the advice given. They are useful in ensuring that your experience counts towards the minimum Part 3 requirements.

It is important to remember that for your Stage 1 and Stage 2 experience to count towards Part 3 you must have your PEDR sheets signed by a mentor (who must be a UK-registered architect or similar co-professional) and by a Professional Studies Advisor (PSA) based in a school of architecture or other provider, such as RIBA North-West or ARCEX. The normal pattern for progression through to Part 3 and its variants is shown in Figure 2.1. The RIBA and ARB requirements changed in 2011 to reflect the variety of valid practical experience and the international and multidisciplinary nature of current architecture practice. The key point to make at this stage is that your 24 months of practical training must now show how you have developed professionally so as to meet the minimum standards and subject areas specified in the Part 3 Criteria (2010).

At Stage 1 most students continue to have some contact with their Part 1 school, but during the period immediately after Part 2 and before enrolling on Part 3 students may no longer be linked to a school. This can pose a problem as, for any post-Part 2 experience to count towards Part 3, students need to be registered with a school or Part 3 provider that will act as a PSA. Many Part 3 students have gained in excess of two years' professional experience in architectural practice before sitting the Part 3 examination. Very few take the examination with only 12 months' post-Part 2 experience. So it is important to think carefully about the experience that you gain and how to document it immediately after Part 2 even if you are not intending to take Part 3 for some time.

If you have trained outside the UK and have enrolled on Part 3 after having passed the ARB Part 1 and Part 2 Prescribed Examinations and/or received recognition of your qualifications from the ARB, you will still need to meet the requirements for practical experience and training. As the PEDR is the recognised way of recording your experience you should familiarise yourself with this method.

Normal model

RIBA Part 1

3 years	Recognised full-time Part 1 degree course

1 year	Stage 1 PEDR

RIBA Part 2

2 years	Recognised full-time Part 2 course

RIBA Part 3

1 year	Stage 2 PEDR + Part 3 course

FIGURE 2.1 Route to registration

Architecture is essentially a practical subject and a minimum of two years' professional experience in the workplace is required in addition to the full-time, part-time or office-based[2] study undertaken to gain Parts 1 and 2. The 12-month Stage 1 period of experience is normally gained immediately after Part 1 and, similarly, the Stage 2 experience after Part 2. Both periods of experience need to be properly recorded using the PEDR and signed by you, your mentor and your PSA. It is not intended to discuss Stage 1 experience in this book, other than to remind you that it must be properly recorded and signed, and that it will be considered by the professional examiners as part of your total work experience.

The key challenge that you face for Part 3 is how to gain the necessary breadth and depth of experience in the shortest possible period of time in order to meet the Part 3 Professional Criteria. The PEDR sample record sheets (which you can view at www.pedr.co.uk) show that, ideally, you should demonstrate that you have gained experience across the Part 3 Criteria and the RIBA Work Stages. The RIBA also recognises that experience in fields other than pure architectural practice is valuable – disaster relief is a good example – but this is not sufficient on its own. The qualification allows you to practise architecture using the title 'architect' and the public, the profession and you yourself need to be reassured that you can do this competently. Not all your competencies will have been gained through direct experience. For example, some may have been gained through shadowing (explained in Chapter 4), a legitimate alternative that can strengthen your skills base. No matter how you acquire your experience, at interview you will need to show that you possess adequate knowledge, understanding and ability to meet the Criteria and to practise competently.

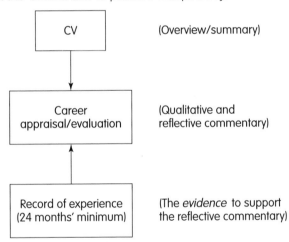

Part 3 professional development and experience: the documentation

Part 3 professional development and experience: the documentation

The Part 3 submission consists of three elements:

> the professional curriculum vitae;
> the PEDR; and
> the career appraisal.

Each of these elements performs a particular function, and understanding how professional examiners use the information you provide on your work experience and how they evaluate your professional development will assist you in preparing fully for interview.

THE CURRICULUM VITAE

The professional curriculum vitae is intended to give the examiners a comprehensive 'snapshot' of your career to date. It is therefore a factual summary of your education and work experience as well as your related interests. It should be complete and follow a simple chronological sequence showing your achievements. It is a professional document that will be read in conjunction with your PEDR and career appraisal and is, therefore, very different in purpose from the curriculum vitae that you would send when applying for a position in an architectural practice, which is often designed to capture the attention of a busy professional. However, Part 3 examiners are qualified architects and think and work with visual information as well as written, factual text. It is also a relevant professional skill to show information in a cogent, persuasive manner using appropriate media. More importantly, feedback from PSAs and examiners confirms that they prefer CVs that combine the factual information of your professional development with images from your portfolio. Therefore, it is worth taking the time to carefully organise the text and images to create a coherent, well-organised and well-presented summary of your educational and professional achievements. You should also limit the detail concerning peripheral interests, which are not relevant to Part 3. A clean driving licence is unlikely to persuade examiners of your professional competence.

Gaps in your CV quite rightly raise questions in the minds of professional examiners. In the first instance gaps might suggest a mistake or omission but, more importantly, they can lead to doubts about the integrity of your professional development. Ideally, the examiners would like to see a seamless career development but, of course, they are aware that life rarely runs smoothly and there might be any number of legitimate reasons for progress to have been interrupted. While you should not dwell on these, it is worth providing a short explanation of any gaps. Otherwise, a simple, factual question at interview could unnerve you, setting the tone for how you answer further, more important questions. It is far better to be able to address these issues in your own time and on paper than under pressure at interview.

Examiners will be interested in your interests outside architecture but these will not affect how they view your overall professional experience and competence to practise, so avoid listing interests that may distract from your general architectural interests and professional development.

Keep the timeline as simple as possible so that examiners can see your progression from one part of your professional education to the next. Drawings or visualisations will be useful in illustrating an aspect of your experience, so ensure that they are legible and relevant.

Do not cut and paste blurb from other sources into your CV. It is not unheard of for material that an employer might have prepared for a different audience to end up in a CV. Some students have been known to overstate their involvement in a project, possibly by mistake, only to find that it works against them in the interview. Do not mistake the polished presentation of some of these documents for real substance – they are often inaccurate, confusing your office role with your professional status. It is not unusual for Part 3 students with job-running skills and responsibilities to be described as the 'project architect'. Avoid any references to the word 'architect', including 'student architect', 'Part 3 architect' and 'junior architect'. To do so indicates ignorance (the title 'architect' is protected) and no little irony, as the whole purpose of undertaking the Part 3 is to earn the right to use the title. Instead, use tried and tested phrases such as 'architectural assistant' or 'Part 3 architectural assistant'. These terms, as well as 'job runner' or 'project manager', are all understood by professional examiners. You may fail as a result of using a protected title inaccurately: it is unprofessional and it does happen.

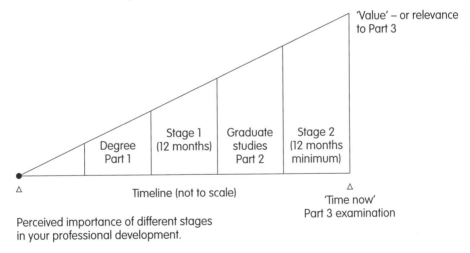

Perceived importance of different stages in your professional development.

THE PEDR[3]

The PEDR is a valuable document for you and your examiners. It is the only place where you can demonstrate, in a standardised way, the projects on which you have worked, the RIBA Work Stages in which you have been actively involved and those you have observed, and how you have progressed explicitly in the context of the Part 3 Criteria. It also covers any other related activities, such as research and non-project-related investigations and the managerial aspects of practice that you have carried out or participated in as a member of a team. In short, it shows in a detailed contemporaneous account how you developed professionally in the workplace, endorsed by your employers and monitored by your PSA. The process for completing the PEDR is covered in detail on the PEDR website. The following section discusses how it is used as a 'product', as part of your Part 3 submission.

The professional examiners will scrutinise your PEDR in detail, in conjunction with your curriculum vitae and the career appraisal, to establish the breadth as well as the depth of your experience. Initially, they will check the basics:

> That it is a true, contemporaneous account and has been reviewed and signed within the recommended periods.
> That it shows where you have worked and for how long. For example, if you have spent 24 months in a series of three-month contract positions, they will be interested to see precisely what you learned in each office and perhaps why you moved on.
> That it shows the type of employer for whom you have worked. If you have worked exclusively within a client organisation, a contractor or a quasi-statutory body that commissions buildings, professional examiners will want to establish your personal involvement and understanding of project processes.
> That it shows your progression: how you have developed your experience and the level of your involvement and responsibility.
> That your mentor is a registered architect or a similarly qualified co-professional and meets the basic requirements of the ARB and RIBA.
> That it shows the time-scale for completion of Part 3 and reveals any significant gaps in your experience.

Once these basics have been covered, the examiners will study the breadth and depth of your experience and the consistency of your record-keeping. If, on questioning at interview, you appear vague about your practical experience this will have two results: it will devalue the accuracy and worth of your PEDR and it will call into question the professionalism of your approach. It is therefore essential to familiarise yourself with the terminology of the PEDR, which mirrors the terms used by architects in professional practice. Examiners may perceive a problem if a significant number of hours are shown to have been spent in one contract administration function: 'instructions', for example. It is vital to discuss how to complete the document with your mentor, to avoid making innocent but unprofessional mistakes that are impossible to rectify at a later date. Mentors cannot be expected to check your PEDR minutely as they will be generalising about your progress rather than cross-referencing every detail. Remember that the professional examiners only have this personal document – they cannot talk to your mentor – and any doubts about the way in which you have completed the PEDR, and hence its accuracy and value, will be difficult to recover retrospectively at interview. Feedback from examiners also highlights the importance of comments from your mentor and PSA. These comments provide evidence of the reflection, dialogue and support of your professional development in the workplace.

RIBA North-West and APSAA have jointly, produced a mentor's guide, an amended version of which is included in Appendix 4. This gives a useful summary of best practice and guidelines for your mentor's engagement with your professional development.

After checking the overview and summary of participation, examiners will look at the range of projects, the types of contract and your detailed record of your achievements over each period, which may form the basis of some early questioning in the interview. You should try to achieve a balance across the complete document. You are not expected to experience every activity in each period.

It follows that if Part 3 examiners do not like gaps they are also concerned if the 'trail runs dry'. If you look at diagram 'x' you will see that the perceived value of your recent experience is higher than at any other time in your professional development. It therefore makes sense to complete the PEDR right up to the time of Part 3 documentary submission.

CERTIFICATES OF PROFESSIONAL EXPIERENCE

'The Certificate of Professional Experience is an alternative online recording format to the standard PEDR, which may be used, with permission from a Part 3 course leader by Part 3 candidates with substantial experience'.

'The candidate must have completed at least 6 years experience... and must have been undertaken outside of full-time academic study for Part 1 and Part 2' [ref. www.pedr.co.uk].

The key words and phrases here are:

> 6 years experience
> substantial experience
> with permission from a Part 3 course leader

You must seek the approval of your Part 3 provider before submitting certificates in lieu of the normal PEDR. "Substantial Experience" also means that you have a position of responsibility and at a senior level.

Because certificates are of limited value to Part 3 examiners in evaluating your experience they must be accompanied by a report and supplementary evidence (see the PEDR website for full details and/or Appendix 6). Furthermore, your Part 3 provider may require you to complete the PEDR for the period you are on the course and up to the oral examination. If you do not then you are up against the 'trail ran dry' problem. You therefore need to think about this carefully: examiners like to see your progression and they prefer to see it in similar format – the PEDR.

If you have any concerns about completing your PEDR, it is worth discussing them with your PSA and your contemporaries. The RIBA Education Department takes an active interest in work-based learning and is also a useful source of help and advice. Completed sample PEDR sheets are available on the PEDR website.

THE CAREER APPRAISAL

The career appraisal (or career evaluation) is the third component of the evidence you present to demonstrate your professional development. The career appraisal is like standing on a hill looking back on the path you've travelled across the landscape of professional development. In a knowledge-based profession, how you think is as important as what you do. The career appraisal is the vehicle for discussing your architectural, educational and professional development in the workplace. It is also a way of demonstrating professional skills and, in particular, the skill of reflection. Whereas the purposes of the CV and the PEDR are reasonably clear, the role of the career appraisal is often misunderstood and therefore you may be led into undervaluing its importance. Its main purpose is to show what you have learned from each experience and how this has informed your continuous development as a professional in architectural practice. It is also an opportunity to demonstrate how your professional experience meets the Part 3 Professional Criteria and is a way of filling gaps in recent experience which are not covered adequately in other parts of your submission. For example, your recent experience might have been to do with production information. This would not be uncommon. You therefore should use the career appraisal as an opportunity to discuss what you have gained by developing a work package through to the detailed production information stage in the context of the project as a whole and also where you have gained other, wider knowledge and experience of other aspects of construction projects and office management. Before getting started it is important that you check the target length of your career appraisal with your Part 3 provider. The word count usually falls within the range of 3,000 to 5,000 words.

The content of the career appraisal

Where do you start? Although you might be tempted to follow Frank Lloyd Wright's example and reminisce about playing with your Froebel blocks by the fireside or your unhealthy interest in Lego – or Minecraft – it is unwise to do so. If you have had an interest in architecture from an early age then say so, but examiners will be looking for your motivation to practise as an architect rather than a general interest. If you follow this approach then the transition will be relevant and could be a useful starting point for your discussion. No two career appraisals will have the same content but they should follow a continuous timeline. The basic elements of this framework should include:

> starting your undergraduate studies (Part 1);
> your Stage 1 experience;
> continuing your architectural education: starting your graduate studies (Part 2);
> your Stage 2 experience;
> the future.

Undergraduate studies

Starting your undergraduate studies (Part 1) A good starting point for your career appraisal might be the issues that influenced your choice of school of architecture from the viewpoint of your interests at the time, perceived strengths and any work experience. Everyone finds the undergraduate experience both difficult and stimulating and there is no harm in discussing this. You should consider your achievements and how your ideas progressed. Exchange programmes give you the opportunity to compare and contrast teaching styles and the student experience from a different perspective.

If you interrupted your studies or changed school, you should not consider this to be an area of weakness or a potential problem. Instead, it is an opportunity to consider the reasons for your decisions.

Stage 1 experience

Your Stage 1 experience Your Stage 1 experience will have taken place some time ago and from a Part 3 perspective it will not appear as valuable now as it did then. (This is, itself, a reflective process.) You should describe the office (or offices) in which you were employed, the type of work and the support you received from the office and how, in turn, you responded to the new work environment. Despite your inevitable tendency to rate this experience as less important because of your current knowledge, it is nevertheless significant. You should describe the projects you worked on, the Work Stages and your level of responsibility. This is also an opportunity to show your increasing understanding of the context of architectural practice as a professional service sitting within the larger construction industry. You will probably have come into contact with other construction professionals – engineers, cost consultants and contractors – for the first time. If you gained your Stage 1 experience outside the UK then examiners will be interested in any comparisons or contrasts that you can make. It is important that you try to capture what you learned: seeing work built, dealing with specialists, gaining competence and learning to ask the right questions.

Graduate studies

Continuing your architectural education: starting your graduate studies (Part 2) For many students Part 2 marks the transition from being interested in architectural design and architecture in its widest sense to choosing to practise architecture as a profession. You will also be in a position to make an informed choice about your school of architecture. Students often change school and if you have done so then you should discuss the positive reasons behind the move, the cultural changes and how you adapted to them. It seems obvious, but it is also useful to mention your major design projects and dissertation subject as well as any achievements and the way in which your interest in architectural practice has developed.

Stage 2 experience

Your Stage 2 experience Your evaluation of this period will be the most important to you personally as it is the most recent and probably the richest in terms of experience, knowledge gained, responsibility and work-based learning. You will also find that this experience is of more value to you than your Stage 1 experience, mainly because you are interpreting it with more precision and with deeper knowledge, as well as a better focus on professional, contractual and regulatory issues.

Meeting the Professional Criteria

You should describe the architectural practices you have worked for in detail. Examiners will be interested in whether you understand the difference between a sole practitioner, a partnership, a limited liability partnership and a limited company. Describe the projects in which you were involved in terms of your role and the different RIBA Work Stages and, where appropriate, areas in which you can demonstrate how you meet the Part 3 Professional

Criteria. If you found that the experience did not meet particular Criteria – say so – rather than feel that you have to make the experience fit. This approach shows that you are interpreting your experience using the professional points of reference that are relevant to Part 3 and which are understandable to the examiners. It also sets the scene for relevant questions at interview. Reflect on that experience and, if appropriate, explain why you moved on. Compare different procedures in different practices in general terms. This comparative discussion is very valuable and as important as giving a comprehensive summary of your experience. It shows your knowledge and understanding as well as your reflective skills.

Filling the gaps

The career appraisal also fulfils the role – if relevant to your experience – of filling gaps in the documentation of your knowledge and experience relating to the Part 3 Criteria. Examiners will read the appraisal in conjunction with the case study when evaluating your experience. If your case study is on a complex management contract and you have only been involved in a limited number of packages, examiners will seek events in your experience that are relevant to PC5 Building Procurement in the Criteria. For example, the 'skills to plan project-related tasks, co-ordinate and engage in design team interaction (and) execute effective contract communication…'.[4] If it is relevant, discuss a suitable project in the career appraisal and highlight your personal involvement. Examiners will sometimes use this material in the interview to explore your understanding of a particular issue: certification, for example. In this way you can:

> show the breadth of your experience;
> prepare the ground for any relevant questions at interview; and
> reassure the examiners of your wider experience.

If you do not make reference to an element of your experience, the examiners will not know about it. At interview they may throw in hypothetical questions to test your knowledge, whereas if questions can be tied to your project experience you will have a better chance of responding positively.

Do not be tempted to invent material or introduce experience into your career evaluation that has not already been documented in the PEDR. Do not try to shape the appraisal so that it seamlessly and comprehensively covers every aspect of the Criteria. Your professional examiners will pick up the inconsistencies in your documentation and sense any artificiality in the way it is presented. This in turn will undermine your professional credibility. You can expect the first questions at interview to be about the inconsistencies rather than what you have learned. Inevitably, this puts you in a defensive position.

Non-traditional experience

The RIBA encourages students, especially during the Stage 1 phase, to gain the widest experience possible. This could mean working in architectural practice outside the UK, working for a contractor, working on a disaster relief project or voluntary work for a charity. Any concerns tend to emerge after Part 2 and one of the issues that students raise consistently is the value of non-UK experience. In the context of international practice this is likely to mean working for a UK-based practice, possibly in an overseas office, exclusively on a project that is not based in the UK. Because you are showing how you meet elements of the Part 3 Criteria through your experiential learning, examiners will give equal credit to this experience and will not penalise you provided you can make some constructive comparisons with UK practice. However, the qualification is a UK one and you must be able to demonstrate your competence in terms of UK practice, to protect the public and yourself and to maintain the reputation of the profession.

Presentation There is no set target for the length of the career appraisal but you should remember that examiners will have many appraisals to read and that careful editing and presentation is considered a professional skill. Illustrations are very useful. Architects are visual people and examiners will welcome a well-presented appraisal that uses material from the projects that you have worked on. You should, however, make it clear if the work presented is not your own.

A powerful way of presenting your experience at each architectural practice is as a colour-coded pie chart (Figure 2.2) or a bar chart that relates to the RIBA Work Stages (Figure 2.3). In this way you can give a graphic summary of the range of your experience.

The future

At the beginning of this section, the career appraisal was likened to climbing a hill and looking back to the starting point of your journey. As registration is the gateway to the profession, examiners will be interested in the view ahead too, to both the near and the distant professional horizons, including your immediate and future professional ambitions. This might include short-term targets for acquiring more knowledge or skills as well as the direction you wish to take in developing your career. Some schools also recommend that your career appraisal includes a Personal Development Plan for the year following registration. This is a useful way of demonstrating 'good practice' and preparing for the future. Examiners and PSAs often describe this as a 'trajectory'. This is a powerful image

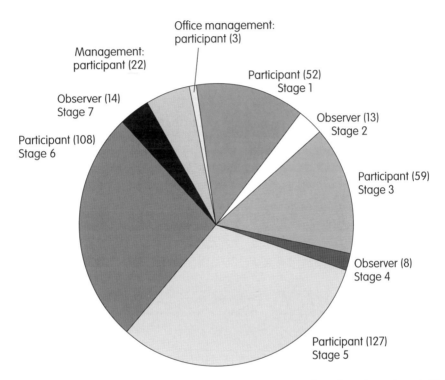

FIGURE 2.2 PEDR quarterly record sheet presented as a pie chart. The chart shows limited experience in Work Satges '0', '2' , '4' and '7'

suggesting an upward path – even a release – that traces your professional development and projects the possible path ahead. To this extent the career appraisal should celebrate your achievements and speculate on your ambitions for the future.

This discussion of your future is, too often, seen as a gesture to future practice and sometimes reads as a 'standalone' statement of intent. Part 3 students also make the mistake that they should write what the examiners want to read. For example: 'I plan to start my own practice in a few years time, when I am ready'.

The discussion about your future should be informed by your past. Your objectives should grow from a recognition of both your strengths and weaknesses as well as your interests and ambitions. It is useful and appropriate to use your previous discussion of architectural practice as a way of focusing on the building blocks for your future career. You will not be able to look ahead and make an accurate prediction about where you will

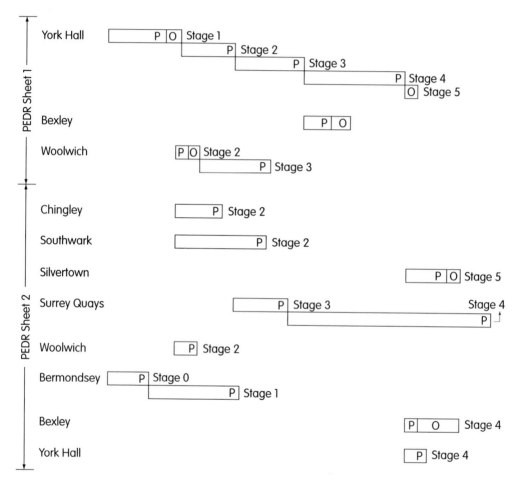

FIGURE 2.3 Two PEDR record sheets covering six months given in bar chart format, showing hours per RIBA Work Stage: P = participant; O = observer. The charts show fragmented experience with little continuity and very little Stage 5 Construction experience. If this continues the student is unlikely to pass Part 3

be in 40 years time but you may be able to look ahead for 4–5 years. Examiners cannot, of course, assess the accuracy of these predictions but they will look for evidence of your professional skills – especially your reflection on your experience and development – as a way of knowing that your competence will grow and that you have the professional skills to meet future challenges.

Summary

This chapter has examined how to compose the CV, approach the PEDR and write the reflective career appraisal. It has also discussed how examiners use this material when preparing themselves for the interview and how early questions in the interview are derived. It is important to remember that your ability to demonstrate the practical application of your knowledge as defined by the Part 3 Professional Criteria and PC1 'professionalism' in particular and your ability to reflect on your experience are essential professional skills. The three components that comprise the evidence of your professional development make a significant contribution to the content of your Part 3 submission and complements and supports your other written work, especially the case study.

WRITTEN EXAMINATIONS
CHAPTER 3

This chapter looks at one of the areas of assessment that is not entirely based on your professional work experience: the written examinations. That said, it is important to understand that the different elements of the Part 3 examination as a whole are closely linked, often overlapping. It is difficult to know which of the different schools of architecture and assessment centres to choose when they structure their Part 3 examination in different ways. It is sensible to investigate how different centres assess candidates to be sure of selecting the one that suits you best. However, the choice is likely to be limited as each centre is assessing the same material to the same standard based on the Criteria.

This chapter aims to:

> *explain the different types of written examinations;*
> *dispel some exam myths;*
> *explain the written examination process in detail;*
> *give useful and practical guidance on what is often perceived as the most difficult and stressful element of Part 3; and*
> *show different approaches to answering a variety of examination questions.*

'Why use written examinations in the context of a professional assessment?'

By the time you consider taking Part 3 you will have left written examinations a long way behind you. It may seem ironic that what is essentially a work-based, professional subject is assessed by a written examination. Written examinations also come with a certain amount of baggage. Thomas Stuttiford, *The Times'* former medical correspondent, recounts a story about his father who served in the trenches during the First World War. He suffered from recurring nightmares for many years afterwards. However, the subject of these nightmares was not the horrors of trench warfare but the fear he experienced while taking his final examinations as a medical student!

Written examinations set under time-limited conditions, often with 'unseen' questions, where candidates have to answer questions under pressure, may seem to be a very artificial process. But in fact it could be argued that professional life functions in just this way. The professional architect seldom has the chance to solve a problem on his or her own terms. It would be very convenient when asked an awkward technical or contractual question in practice, whether by a client, colleague, consultant or contractor, to be able to reply that you will get back to them in a few days, after reviewing the standard texts, maybe taking some further advice and balancing the arguments and facts. The answer might be a good one but by then the problem will have moved on. An architect needs to be in the position of possessing adequate, appropriate knowledge and experience to make a realistic, accurate professional judgement quickly and with assurance. The solution does not have to be perfect, but it should be one that other architects would make under similar circumstances. Boris Johnson, the politician and journalist, observed that written examinations are more like 'real life' than written assignments and continuous assessment. In an article entitled: 'Exams work because they're scary'[1] he observed, tongue-in-cheek, that we all have to work under pressure and to deadlines:

> 'people's jobs are becoming more and more like time-limited exams. We live in an economy increasingly dominated by the service sector, and everywhere you look people are required to cram at the last minute and then perform…. You need the fear to push up your brain's RPM, and it is only when the flywheel is humming that you suddenly see the connections and problems disappear; and there comes a magic moment when the clouds in your head all part at once, and you can see straight up to the stars.'

The different types of written examination

In order to combat the perceived artificiality of time-limited written examinations, different universities and examination centres use different formats for Part 3. Most of these written examinations are 'problem-based', using a range of scenarios. A very small minority has dispensed with written examinations altogether and relies on intensive coursework and written assignments but, generally, all Part 3 examinations have at least one significant written examination at the heart of their assessment.

The different types of written examination are as follows:

1. time-limited, 'unseen';
2. time-limited, 'unseen', 'open book';
3. time-limited, 'unseen', based on a scenario circulated to candidates in advance;
4. time-limited, 'unseen', short knowledge-based questions;
5. office-based, 'unseen', based on a scenario and taken over a day or a number of days.

The key vehicle for the written examination is the 'project scenario'. The examination paper is essentially problem-based and practical rather than discursive and theoretical.

Scenario-based written examinations serve a number of functions. For the examiner, they allow a relatively standard set of subjects to be covered in a variety of ways. Different topics can be covered to different depths and linked to different subject areas. At the heart of the assessment strategy is the application of relevant knowledge to reach a conclusion. Often, as in architectural practice, there is a range of answers to one question. Therefore, examiners attempt to frame questions that will allow candidates to examine the process of reasoning, supported by appropriate knowledge rather than arriving at a single answer. The method of approaching these questions will be discussed in detail below.

The developing project scenario is also a useful means of testing different areas of knowledge. Therefore, in order to make papers more readily understandable the scenario usually has a simple timeline that generally follows the RIBA Plan of Work: starting with inception and feasibility and ending with post-completion issues such as patent and latent defects and the final account. In this way candidates can be assessed in the key areas of the architect's appointment, regulatory issues such as town planning and health and safety, procurement, contract choice and contract administration.

Papers may also have multiple scenarios. Multiple scenarios are used to cover areas that do not fit easily into a single project timeline. Therefore candidates can expect other 'events' to be introduced, such as health and safety or party wall issues, for example.

Finally, there are areas of knowledge such as office management and the development of the architectural profession that do not lend themselves to scenario-based questions. Examiners approach these in two ways:

> They will introduce more speculative discussion-type questions, sometimes based around a fictional lunchtime CPD event or briefing of the 'year-out' student about relevant project-based or professional issues.
> They will set another, wholly knowledge-based, examination.

Both these assessment strategies are used. The first type allows more discursive answers based on sound knowledge and an ability to edit knowledge to target the question. Subject areas might include wider construction industry issues such as the impact of off-site manufacturing or the role of the project manager. The second strategy relies on 'quick-fire' questions and a clear understanding of what is required. Candidates often have only five or six minutes to answer each of the questions, which are sometimes very detailed. Typical areas of questioning might include adjoining owners' rights and responsibilities, the Building Regulations, as well as property and land law subjects such as easements and restrictive covenants. These require a basic knowledge and understanding of the key subject areas.

Dispelling myths about written examinations

Written examinations in general have developed their own set of myths over the years. Some may contain a grain of truth but it is important to realise that they mostly do not apply to the Part 3 examination.

'FAILING WILL RUIN YOUR LIFE'

You may have felt this when sitting GCSEs or 'A' levels and, indeed, these two sets of examinations are important gateways to higher education and, in the case of the architectural student, a professional career, but professional examinations are different. There is always an option to resit and almost all students pass the second time around: not because they are assessed more leniently but because they have understood the required level of knowledge and mastered the required techniques (see below). Failure, followed by debriefing and feedback from an experienced examiner or Part 3 tutor and reflection on your own performance, can be a very rewarding experience. Candidates generally do not feel under the same amount of pressure and the process is one of 'topping up' and fine-tuning rather than starting from scratch.

'SOME PEOPLE ARE BETTER THAN OTHERS AT SITTING EXAMINATIONS: MY STRENGTH IS IN THE WORKPLACE NOT THE EXAMINATION HALL'

This may be true of a very small minority of candidates and it is true that, very occasionally, a candidate will produce an uncharacteristically stunning performance in a written examination. These instances are, however, very rare and it is reasonable to assume that we will all perform in much the same way. The significant majority of candidates pass and they do so because they have prepared thoroughly and professionally. It is also true that in the workplace you generally work in teams comprising differing levels of competence and knowledge. However, the test of the professional architect is an *individual* test and assumes that you will be in a position to work autonomously or at least to guide others who do not have the benefit of your specific knowledge and skills.

'YOU NEED A PHOTOGRAPHIC MEMORY'

This is a common misconception. The section on examination technique below considers ways to improve your performance. As designers you will have finely tuned visual skills and there are ways to harness those skills to good effect. In many cases the written examinations are 'open book', so remembering vast chunks of town planning law and JCT standard contractual terms and conditions is not an issue. In fact, it could be argued that relying solely on your memory in a professional context is dangerous both because your memory is neither perfect nor comprehensive and because the information we rely on changes almost daily. It is the ability to update your knowledge base conscientiously and know what to retrieve and when that is the valued professional skill. However, just to confuse matters, it would be fair to conclude that you need a detailed knowledge of some areas, if only to know where to look for further information. Also, to an extent, it is the *type* rather than the *amount* of knowledge that we hold and update that helps to define our value as a professional.

'YOU NEED TO KNOW EVERYTHING ABOUT THE SUBJECT TO PASS'

In a professional context this is clearly a non-starter, for the reasons touched on above. However, it is difficult to judge how much you need to know and in what depth. This challenge applies in the workplace as well as in the examination hall but, unlike GCSEs, 'A' levels and some undergraduate examinations, the Part 3 examination assesses the breadth and depth of your professional knowledge and your ability to apply that knowledge to difficult problems in the context of a lifelike scenario.

'WRITTEN EXAMINATIONS ARE FULL OF TRICK QUESTIONS'

It may sometimes feel that the subject area of a particular question is rather opaque. Questions may appear to be overly complex, touching on too many areas. However, in drafting papers, examiners deliberately phrase questions in a way that allows you to show and apply your professional knowledge rather than your clairvoyant techniques. The task facing examiners is to draft questions that are challenging and which test a set of professionally agreed areas of knowledge in a seemingly new way. Occasionally they fail in that task by setting overly difficult questions. In such cases two things can occur. First, given the choice, candidates may choose not to answer that particular question. Often it is the weaker student, whose choices are already limited, that answers it, with predictable results. Second, the examiners may moderate the answers. This is a process whereby the examiners recognise collectively that the question needs to be marked in a different way.

'THERE IS A RIGHT ANSWER AND A WRONG ANSWER'

Well … yes and no. Questions are set in order to assess particular areas of knowledge. However, there are also questions which are trying to elicit a range of answers. These include questions concerning procurement and contract choice or different types of architectural practice, where no 'right' answer exists. In these questions it is the process of discussion and analysis and the range of relevant options considered that will be assessed rather than the 'rightness' of a single solution.

'YOU HAVE TO CRAM UNTIL YOU DROP'

You will realise fairly rapidly that studying for a professional examination and working full time, together with all the other complexities of a professional adult life, is very different from full-time academic study. Cramming is probably not an option or at least is a very high-risk strategy for preparing for complex, problem-based examinations.

What makes a bad answer

If candidates can understand the factors that make a bad answer and avoid these then success should be the result. The factors that contribute to poor answers are:

> poor time management;
> poor structure and presentation;
> not answering the question or answering a different question;
> giving too much, often extraneous, detail or too little;
> stating standardised knowledge and not applying it to the problem;
> generalisation – failing to show the process.

These shortcomings are discussed in detail below.

Examination technique

'Examination technique' causes much discussion. It is clear that only a tiny minority of candidates are naturally (or unnaturally) very good at answering time-limited questions. Also, and importantly, in a professional context it is very difficult to sustain this performance across a range of examination papers and different methods of assessment.

Judging the right level of detail and how to apply it is difficult and comes only with practice. It involves understanding the level of knowledge required as much as applying any particular technique.

It could be argued that there is no such thing as 'examination technique': it is only a different application of professional life skills, such as working under pressure and providing succinct answers to specific questions.

A good start to your preparation is to join or form a revision group. The group should meet regularly (every week if possible) and try to be reasonably disciplined about what it covers. It is also a good opportunity to pool resources, exchange copies of articles and simply offer mutual support. As the ability to reflect on your performance as a professional is an important life skill, preparing topics for discussion in a friendly, non-adversarial environment and reflecting on how you have approached a topic or problem is an important process. Remember to stay focused and be critical of yourself and others in the group in a constructive way. Identifying gaps is often more difficult than finding weaknesses so try to look expansively on each subject area and from different perspectives too.

Critical success factors

All the following factors are important in producing relevant and clear answers to written examination questions.

TIME MANAGEMENT

Most candidates will have arrived at Part 3 having mastered written examinations, at least at an undergraduate level. However some, who have been assessed by coursework and assignments, will not have honed the necessary skills. In any event you are unlikely to have taken a formal examination for a number of years. The context and preparation for your study, as well as the subject areas, will be very different. Your life generally is likely to be more complex and your level of professional knowledge and understanding will be higher. Most Part 3 written examinations are considered, rightly, to be at Master's degree level rather than undergraduate (Part 1) or graduate (Part 2) levels. In particular, the calls on your time are likely to be much greater than at any other time in your life and you must find ways of fitting in study on top of everything else.

Time management starts with careful planning, prioritisation and self-discipline. It should start with the targeted reading associated with each lecture topic during the course. Choosing when and how to read around topics and discovering what interests you is essential. Remember that you cannot cram for these examinations – or if you do, it is a very high-risk strategy that exchanges short-term recall for in-depth understanding. You are likely to be found out later in the assessment process, at the oral examination in particular.

Step 1   Plan in the macro environment – using sources of information

Seek out the key texts and pre-plan your library visits or web-based searches. Unfortunately, many reading lists tend to be too detailed. Most lecturers are experts in their field and, when asked a specific question, will tend to give a very detailed response which would be impossible to repeat under time-limited examination conditions. A useful tip is to ask recent past students what they found most useful. The book catalogues produced by RIBA bookshops and the other professional publishers also make a good starting point.

There is a relatively limited range of accessible, standard texts relevant to Part 3. Remember that books have a long gestation period and may even be out of date shortly after publication. Also, collections of contributions by experts brought together by editors – though accurate – tend to reflect the interests of the contributors and may not give a balanced or comprehensive point of reference of the subject. Therefore, do not rely on a single source – look at different texts on a given subject – and use your critical skills to evaluate the information. This critical appraisal will improve your knowledge and understanding of the subject area.

Make sure that you set aside time for reading the legal and practice pages of the professional architectural and construction industry journals. The *Architects Journal*, the *RIBA Journal* and *Building* are useful because they tend to concentrate on the practical issues rather than becoming side-tracked (in terms of relevance to Part 3) into design or partisan issues. Specialist journals such as the *International Construction Law Review* or the more widely available *Journal of Construction Law* have relatively short articles by experts on particular topics. Because the journals have much shorter lead-in times they can respond to new topics far faster than book publishers. In reality the depth of knowledge and analysis shown in the specialist journals is greater than that required for Part 3 but they will give you an insight into the complexity of construction law in particular.

Visiting your nearest local authority development and building control departments either physically or online and looking at some planning applications and collecting the free advice aimed at consumers as well as professionals can be extremely worthwhile. It gives you a flavour of the process as well as giving succinct advice on procedures. Also, make use of web-based professional and construction industry-wide resources. Local authority, government agency and government department websites are often clearer, more succinct and more up to date than many of the standard textbooks when it comes

44

to the regulatory framework, health and safety and industry-wide initiatives. For example, the planning portal (www.planningportal.gov.uk) gives access to the latest planning procedures, a comprehensive glossary of relevant terms and more detailed information on correct planning policy. The site also covers the Building Regulations in detail. The Health and Safety Executive website (www.hse.gov.uk) provides similar information on the CDM Regulations and approved codes of practice. The ARB and RIBA websites are the main sources for codes of conduct and standards. The 'high street' banks are also a good source for examples of business plans and practice finance models.

Step 2 Plan your revision for each examination in detail

Detailed planning is a way of managing the conflicting demands and complexity of your professional and personal life. A useful method is to set out in detail the six-week period running up to the written examinations. Plot 'non-negotiable' events: work, family and social commitments. Then set aside other periods for study and revision. From the course syllabus, lecture series titles, course handbook or past examination papers, plot the different subject areas, leaving larger periods of time such as weekends for the more complex topics such as JCT contracts or methods of dispute resolution. Set aside time to look at past papers and some 'float time' to take account of the unexpected, including encountering a difficult topic as well as unexpected social demands.

Agree times to meet with your revision group – if you have one – and the topics that you are going to cover.

Use this plan to negotiate with work, friends and family. Monitor your progress. Expect that you will not keep to your plan and be aware that it is very difficult to catch up once you are behind schedule. A comparatively small amount of time invested now will reap great rewards later.

Step 3 The final days before the written examinations

By this time you should be clear about the topics with which you are most comfortable. You can choose to accept that there are certain areas in which you will be weaker or use these final days to work on those topics. Using your personal assessment, plan your time *in the examination* ahead of the examination. This applies to work-based examinations taken over one or two days as much as for the more conventional 2–3 hour time-limited examinations.[2] Most scenario-based examination papers have a natural chronology, often modelled on the RIBA Plan of Work. It may make sense to follow that chronology rather than choose your strongest topic first.

Step 4   In the examination

Read the paper carefully, check and make sure that you follow the rubric, allow time for reading again and planning, then set down when you are going to start and finish answering a question. In 'open book' examinations, factor in time for referring to standard texts, JCT or other standard forms of contract, codes and agreements. Allow a short period of time for reading over your answers.

Write these target times against the questions on the examination paper. Stick to this religiously, even if you have not finished a question. Be aware that you will tend to write more, and for longer, on your strongest topics. Try not to fall into the trap of going over your target time – it is impossible to make up time, especially on your weaker subjects.

Step 5   After the examination

Do not review your performance in detail – yet. Concentrate on the next examination.

None of this advice is mind-bogglingly complex, it is just plain common sense. However, at the heart of the preparation process lies the professional skill of prioritisation of effort over a finite period. You will need to make choices and compromises. You may even need to explain the commitment and negotiate time off from your office.

Time management is crucial. On a level playing field and with equal abilities, the candidate that plans carefully will do better than the one that does not.

STRUCTURE AND PRESENTATION

Like clients, contractors and consultants, examiners respond to good structure and presentation. All examiners recognise that the standard of your performance is likely to drop under time-limited conditions. For this reason questions are often phrased in such a way as to give a ready structure to your answer. Where possible, follow that structure. It should make the question more straightforward to answer and simpler for the examiner to mark. You might wish to combine parts, but if you do, try to be consistent and remember that this might be easier for you but harder for the examiner who is trying to mark consistently across every script.

Follow guidelines carefully. Look for the operative word or phrase. For example, if the questions says 'list' or 'set out' it is testing your knowledge of the subject. If the question asks you to write a letter, do follow a letter format. If the question asks for a 'short report', this is an invitation to give the answer a coherent report structure that avoids the more discursive structure of essays. Students sometimes complain that the question is asking the impossible. For example, they might be asked to prepare a complex fee proposal in a letter format within 25 minutes, which is a tall order. Examiners will accept that this is an artificial demand, but they are looking for a practical response to a problem that is neither formulaic nor overly academic. They will be very aware that your answer will not be polished but you should still try your best to produce as comprehensive an answer as possible.

If you are asked to discuss options and make recommendations, do just that. Write an introduction that sets out the issues, follow it with a detailed discussion of the options (see below) and finish with a short conclusion and a set of recommendations.

In any answer you should be aware of the 'law of diminishing returns'. In the context of Part 3, the law states that as your effort increases the marginal returns diminish. In the context of a time-limited written examination this means two things. First, the longer you spend answering a question the harder it becomes to add significantly to what you have written in response to that question. Second, the longer the time spent on one question the less time is available to answer the next. In the unreal environment of the examination hall a five or six minute overrun on four out of five questions means that you are unlikely to answer the last question at all, which means that the maximum mark available to you is 80 per cent, not 100 per cent. Also, examiners drafting and marking questions broadly follow the rule of diminishing returns too. Candidates can pick up marks relatively easily up to the pass mark but it becomes increasingly hard to gain full marks. Universities might promote high achievement in the form of a Merit Award or a Commendation, but the profession is merely looking for an agreed standard of competence.

The law of diminishing returns is a natural rule. In the workplace we all know that we can produce a reasonable specification or drawing package in good time. It is making it comprehensive that seems to take an eternity, by which time the pressure to deliver is increasing and the motivation and interest is decreasing. It is, perhaps, for this reason that it is not uncommon for some work at tender stage to remain incomplete but sufficient 'for pricing purposes'. Unfortunately, we cannot compensate for insufficient information in the examination hall by working later or longer: that option is not available.

ANSWERING THE QUESTION … OR NOT

Failing to answer the question may seem an unlikely problem, but it does happen. To take an analogy from an office situation, if you are asked a specific question but give a very good answer to another, possibly similar, question you might be met by polite but baffled silence. In the written examination, questions tend to be phrased in such a way as to indicate the particular type of answer that the examiners expect. Of course, under examination pressure we are all prone to misread the question. However, examiners are expecting accuracy and relevance. Reading the 'wrong answer' will leave the examiner wondering if you knew anything at all and unable to give you the benefit of the doubt.

To confuse the issue further, there may not be one 'right' answer but a range of relevant answers. This is particularly true of questions on procurement or contract choice or different types of practice. How you arrive at the answer and the process that you have followed is often more important than the answer itself. Part 3 examiners want to see the robustness of your reasoning as well as the depth of your knowledge. If you can discuss different options, discount some and propose perhaps one or two, with clear reasoning, then that is probably as much as an office or a client would expect and therefore it will satisfy the examiner.

THE RIGHT LEVEL OF DETAIL AND CONTENT

One of the major concerns of Part 3 students is the depth as well as the breadth of the knowledge that they must have to pass the examination.

In an evolving professional context it is impossible to know everything at any one time. In a holistic profession such as architecture it is also important to be able to source other expertise as well as to apply your own knowledge to a particular problem. As is to be expected, there are no easy examination answers.

Part 3 questions often force you to focus and apply your knowledge to a particular problem. It is the judgement you use in this process as much as the knowledge you possess that is being assessed.

Because examinations are time-limited, the questions restrict the knowledge that you can draw on and apply. This highlights the difficulty of using comprehensive reference books (which are written for the architectural office first rather than as student textbooks). For revision and in the examination itself, relying on the information they contain can lead to answers that do not get to the point quickly enough. Remember also that standard reference books are frequently out of date, even when recently published. They are also generally a collection of works by different specialists whose editors may be reluctant to shed detail even when it is not absolutely relevant.[3]

STANDARD KNOWLEDGE

Preparation for Part 3 requires the acquisition and maintenance of a standard or 'core' knowledge. However, architecture is a practical profession and the value of your professional knowledge lies in its appropriate application. The challenge for the person drafting the paper is to ask the candidate to draw on relevant knowledge and apply it. As discussed above, managing, drawing on and applying the right level of information is precisely what is being tested. Examiners will give credit for your knowledge but if it is not related to the problem at hand it will be unlikely to be sufficient to pass. The methodologies discussed below should assist in achieving the right balance of knowledge and application.

GENERALISATION – FAILING TO SHOW THE PROCESS

This can be seen as a follow-on issue from the standard knowledge problems discussed above. However, it differs in several significant ways. The kind of generalisation to watch out for may give a solution to a problem but fails to provide any context or show the process that allowed you to arrive at that solution. It lacks the crucial steps of considering and disregarding alternative solutions before arriving at an answer. Needless to say, it is especially important to avoid generalisations in the context of scenario-based problems where there is no single 'right' answer but a range of answers. The reasons for selecting the preferred option should be substantiated. If you fail to follow this process the examiner is left wondering whether you understand or can justify the answer you have given, or whether you are even aware of the alternatives and their respective strengths. In the context of Part 3, procurement and contract choice are fertile subjects to which to apply this evaluation process. Contractual problems rarely have a single answer and thus lend themselves to this approach. The robustness and completeness of your thinking processes using relevant knowledge to arrive at an appropriate answer are as important as the answer itself.

Typical examination question formats

This section is not intended to be a standalone guide to Part 3 written examinations or a substitute for acquiring appropriate knowledge. The examples here have been devised to highlight what examiners are looking for and to give you a set of tools for approaching examination questions. Because most Part 3 written examinations are scenario-based there are unlikely to be any 'model answers'. An approach that blends appropriate knowledge and its application will be considered here rather than set-piece answers. In any event, set-piece answers where 'one size fits all' are unlikely to succeed. This section will also discuss how to use sources in 'open book' examinations.

First, it is useful to review the different types of written examination because they use specific techniques or a mix of techniques. Although they all have much in common, there are minor differences. For the purposes of discussing examination technique, the different types can be re-categorised as follows:

> time-limited: short questions;
> time-limited: long questions, typically 'open book' and scenario-based;
> office-based: one to two days, 'open book' and scenario-based.

SHORT QUESTION EXAMINATIONS

Time-limited short question papers ask candidates to answer a large number of questions in a relatively short time. Typically, this may mean 15–20 questions in 1½–2 hours, with a very limited choice of question. These are purely knowledge-based examinations testing basic and detailed knowledge across the Part 3 Criteria. They are normally used in conjunction with more discursive, scenario-based papers.

Preparation for this type of examination requires a broad knowledge of most topics. They might appear to lend themselves to memorising large amounts of factual information at a superficial level but this alone is unlikely to succeed due to the breadth of the subject areas and the level of detail required. Success therefore requires a good depth of understanding built up over a considerable time. Past papers are a useful starting point in understanding the structure of the questions and how subjects are organised. They also give a feel for the level of knowledge required. It is likely that many of the questions will come up in various forms repeatedly as there is a finite number of questions that can be asked, especially on regulatory issues.

The answers to these questions are factual. In four or five minutes it is almost impossible to add anything more than basic knowledge of a given subject. The challenge is therefore primarily a matter of sufficient preparation and good time management.

Time-limited, scenario-based examinations can be 'open book' or 'closed book'. Neither type of examination is intended to be a pure test of memory. In the 'open book' examination, questions are likely to require you to draw on a range of resources and apply them to particular problems. The complexity of architectural practice and construction means that it is impossible to memorise the vast amounts of data involved accurately. Examiners recognise this and in 'scenario-based' papers the questions encourage the use of available resources. The 'closed book' type of paper is designed to be more discursive, to consider wider issues and to rely on reasoned arguments backed up by a sound professional knowledge. Questions either fall into the 'compare and contrast' category or contain a detailed problem that requires the use of basic concepts to understand and resolve a set of issues. Most Part 3 written examination papers fall into the 'open book' category, being practical, problem-based questions. You are, therefore, usually allowed to take in unmarked standard forms of contract, the architect's appointment, codes and standards and possibly standard texts that you might refer to in an office. By extension you might be allowed to take in any published material.

'OPEN BOOK' TECHNIQUES

One of the challenges you will face in the 'open book' type of examination is how to use the sources effectively. If you are forced to look up a contractual problem to do with delays to the completion date in the standard handbooks or forms of contract you will quickly experience an information overload. The information is rarely tailored to your particular problem or edited for quick reference. On the contrary, the standard handbooks and forms of contract try to cover all eventualities. Also, some standard texts can appear too formulaic, presenting a 'one-size-fits-all' approach to, for example, contract selection that will lead you to fall into the trap of 'generalisation'. Also, all this retrieval of information takes time. Having found what you want, you then need to read it, locate the relevant point and then apply it or, at worst, copy it.

As a matter of best practice, you should always cite your source; not to do so is to risk being accused of passing it off as your own work. In a time-limited examination, these factors are obviously critical. You also need to recognise that examiners, as seasoned architectural practitioners, are going to be more familiar with the material than you are and will spot material copied from standard texts and give you very little credit for it.

The 'open book' format examination is not as straightforward as it first appears. The effective use of sources has a number of facets. Think about your information needs in the office. A building performance regulation is a good example, or perhaps 'means of escape' distances. When you look at the texts there are different levels of information with an inherent hierarchy of detail. If you are familiar with the concepts, finding the exact detail will still take time. If you are not, it will take considerably more time to navigate your way around the levels until you retrieve the required information. If you are not clear about the problem and unfamiliar with the material you may never find the solution without assistance. The same applies in Part 3. It is important to be familiar with the standard texts, knowing the subject headings and where to find them. This becomes complicated with standard forms of contract which also cross-refer to other conditions of the contract. (The exception to this is the NEC family of forms, in which the NEC drafting committee deliberately avoided cross-referencing and repetition.) You do not need to memorise the detail but you need to know how to find it quickly. Subject to the examination rules, you may be able to follow a technique used by barristers in court who operate under similar pressure with very large amounts of information – that is to 'signpost' parts of contracts or agreements with different coloured tags for quick reference. However, you must check that this is acceptable first.

Having found the information, how do you use it effectively? It is worth taking a quick step back to consider the question: Why are you looking for the information? If you are unfamiliar with the nature of the problem and are looking for a standard answer then you are unlikely to be able either to sift or edit the information or to apply it to the problem. Examiners see this all the time in response to detailed questions. For example, if a question concerns health and safety regulations and the answer goes into lots of detail – some relevant, some not – typically using multiple bullet points, the examiner will quickly understand that, although the candidate has located a relevant seam, he or she is frantically mining it indiscriminately. It is a 'scatter gun' approach where only some of the shot will hit the target. From the examiner's point of view there is no evidence that the candidate is using the information *effectively* and applying it to the problem.

You may use comprehensive detail legitimately provided it is in support of a general view about, for example, the Designer's duties in the CDM Regulations. To do so demonstrates that you understand the problem and know where to look for the detail and can then apply or target it effectively. You are using the reference material to give detail and authority to your answer, using the 'open book' to reinforce your general and specific professional knowledge by applying it to the question. For example, in a question about the functions of the architect under the terms of a construction contract you could refer to the periodic valuation of works and the issue of interim certificates. Supporting this with a reference to the relevant contractual condition gives your answer more substance and shows that you are familiar with this aspect of the contract.

This approach of using detail to support your analysis and commentary rather than relying entirely on the source as your verbatim answer is effective not only in terms of content or quality but also in terms of time. The standard texts should be used in a supporting, secondary role. Inevitably, this needs practice and it is worth thinking through problems or attempting old examination questions and listing the documents to which you might want to refer. You will see that a pattern quickly emerges. Preparation and practice are the keys to using sources effectively in 'open book' examinations. It is also very important to organise your sources in a way that allows you to retrieve detailed information quickly.

OFFICE-BASED EXAMINATIONS

Office-based examinations are hybridised versions of the time-limited written examination. They combine the formality of the written paper with a degree of reality taken from an evolving imaginary office scenario or scenarios, often with a significant degree of complexity and detail. Some universities will not allow them for quality control reasons and the obvious prospect of plagiarism or cheating. Others maintain that the office-based examination, taken over one or two days, is closer to the architect's experience in practice and therefore is a more accurate assessment of performance in a professional context. The advantage to the candidate is that the pressure and apparent artificiality of the three-hour examination is removed. However, the longer period of time available generally means that the questions are more complex and the answers are expected to be more detailed. There is also a tendency to 'throw in the kitchen sink' and fall victim to the 'open book' tendency to mistake the quantity of information for quality. Understandably, examiners can become frustrated wading through lots of extraneous detail that might show evidence of knowing where to look but not where to stop. In the effort to simulate the office environment, questions often include complex scenarios and an exchange of correspondence with a considerable amount of detail. Interestingly, the techniques for both the time-limited and the office-based examination settings are similar and candidates in one kind fail as frequently as in the other.

Types of question and how to answer them

The questions in 'short question' examinations fall into different categories. To understand why, it is worth investigating what the examiners are trying to get at. They want to test essential professional knowledge and, to a lesser extent, judgement in a consistent way and to a level that is acceptable to the profession and to the public that 'consumes' architectural services. The written examinations tend to be more efficient at assessing whether you possess knowledge and understanding of a wide range of issues to a satisfactory level than they are at testing professional judgement or detailed potential scenarios. More in-depth detail is tested in the case study. Therefore questions fall into the following categories:

> knowledge-based;
> problem/scenario-based;
> issue-based.

KNOWLEDGE-BASED QUESTIONS

Questions are typically either 'open' or 'closed'. 'Open' questions do not invite a single answer but rather a range of possible answers that combine facts and apply them. 'Closed' questions tend to require a particular response: a targeted, factual answer. Both types of question lend themselves to a particular form of answer.

> An example of an 'open' question is: A mixed-use scheme in the office has received town planning consent and you have been instructed to proceed with design development. The site must be cleared and any decontamination dealt with before construction starts. This is likely to take six months. Write a short report explaining the procurement routes available for both the site clearance and the construction of the scheme and give your recommendations for the most appropriate form of contract for the project. The development will be in two phases. Each phase has a budget of £8 million.
> An example of a 'closed' question is: The six-month Rectification Period on a recently completed office refurbishment project has expired. Explain the actions you should take under the terms of a JCT Standard Building Contract With Quantities.

The challenge of knowledge-based questions is to know the amount of detail required to achieve the pass mark. For example, the question: 'Explain the main characteristics of a contract under English Law' needs a clear, factual response. Under time-limited conditions examiners are looking for perhaps five or six basic points about this strand of common law. Therefore an answer might cover the following points:

> Simple contracts are signed by the parties to the contract. Examples include the agreement between architect and client such as the RIBA's Forms of Agreement and between employer and contractor such as one of the JCT family of contracts.
> To be valid contracts must meet certain characteristics: offer and acceptance, consideration, legality, capacity.
> Contracts are essentially private but must comply with certain statutes. Examples include the Misrepresentation Act 1967 and the Unfair Contract Terms Act 1977.

> In the context of construction contracts, the contractor agrees to perform certain functions for an agreed cost within an agreed timescale with interim payments made by the employer. The architect may administer the terms of the contract and settle claims under the contract.
> Liability under a simple contract is limited to six years.
> The doctrine of privity of contract establishes that only the parties to the contract can sue or be sued for damages.

Depending on the nature of the question, the answer might expand on some of the following points: the complexities of construction contracts and, in particular, the problem of rights of third parties, the use of collateral warranties and the effects of the Contract (Rights of Third Parties) Act 1999. You do not need to remember exact titles of statutes or their dates. It would be very unusual if you could recall them (for example, the Third Party would be sufficient) but they have been included here for completeness.

A question about town planning procedures, in contrast, would require more specific detail. You need to include the necessary statutes and you should know the processes required to make different types of planning application and appeals. For example, an answer to a question about making planning applications would probably include the following:

> Early consultation or 'pre-submission' meetings; reference to up-to-date local authority documents; the effect of the NPPF on local policy.
> The effect of national policies such as flood defences or renewable energy targets.
> A comment about the choices available – outline or full – and the possible reasons why you might not have a choice in certain circumstances.
> A summary of the forms and the correct notice.
> The information to be provided.
> The role of design statements and environmental impact assessments.
> Time required for consultation and reaching a decision.

Depending on the question, the answer might consider the role and effect of statutory Section 106 Agreements, the Community Infrastructure Levy and appeal procedures.

PROBLEM/SCENARIO-BASED QUESTIONS

Most written examination papers use problem/scenario-based questions but in a variety of formats. In general, time-limited examinations use relatively simple scenarios with a limited number of possible events. In office-based examinations there is the opportunity to simulate reality more closely by including letters and faxes that must be answered, built around the basic scenario. In both cases the questions are based on professional, regulatory and contractual problems, usually following a typical project life cycle from inception to completion.

To complicate matters, scenario-based questions will invariably contain some knowledge-based questions at their heart.

A poor answer will include all the pitfalls mentioned already: containing insufficient or too much information, being too generalised, using textbook sources indiscriminately. Examiners expect you to apply your knowledge to the imperfect information supplied to arrive at the best possible answer in the circumstances. The process, your explanation of that process and the sources that you rely on to inform your recommendations are generally more important than the recommendation itself. Examiners will give you credit for the completeness of the process, even if the final recommendation in your answer is inappropriate.

All problem-based questions raise the dilemma of how best to demonstrate the knowledge you possess without it seeming irrelevant. In this instance examiners are looking for your judgement in the application of your knowledge.

Take, for example, a question that asks you to set out the key issues relating to the scenario site, which might be a brownfield site on the outskirts of a town, surrounded by industrial sheds and/or a late 20th-century housing estate. You will see that a bullet-pointed list is not appropriate as an answer. The examiners are asking you to think about the issues relating to that site. Although this is specifically not an invitation to show off your full understanding of town planning and land law, you are expected to demonstrate how these matters fit into the particular case. The best way of doing so is to gather together all the issues that might affect your answer, even if they are discounted later. For example, you will want to:

> set out brief characteristics of the site;
> make reference to key development drivers such as the Local Plan and note early consultation with the local authority;
> comment on factors that are unlikely to apply in this instance, such as Conservation Areas and Listed Building Consent for alterations/demolition;

> highlight the possible uses and change of use;
> highlight the possibility of site contamination and its effects;
> mention other possible relevant issues, such as rights of way, possible easements and restrictive covenants;
> give your recommendations for further investigation and action.

In each case you should give a relevant example. You can meet the challenge of demonstrating your knowledge of a particular issue by saying that it does *not* apply, for example Conservation Areas and Listed Buildings Consent. There is a large overlap with how to answer the purely knowledge-based questions but the difference lies in the idea of editing and prioritising your knowledge to meet the demands of the question.

Another example, similar to the example of the 'open question', might be giving advice on contract selection for a particular project, for example a new-build single-storey building for an experienced client. The site needs to be cleared first and there is likely to be some specialist design input. The budget, including site clearance, is approximately £3 million.

The answer requires the same use of applied knowledge but it is much more open-ended: there is a range of appropriate and inappropriate options. One approach by which you can both demonstrate the knowledge you have and apply it to arrive at a set of appropriate recommendations is detailed below:

1. Make any assumptions that seem appropriate. For example, a traditional procurement route with the architect as lead consultant, or keep these options open, leaving design and build as a possibility.
2. Briefly set out your interpretation of the characteristics of the project and its effects. Consider the contractual risks. However, you will not receive any marks for repeating information already detailed in the question.
3. Site clearance might be dealt with in one of two ways: as a separate contract or as part of the main contract. If you choose the first option you should explain the benefits: early start, contamination and asbestos identified early, risk reduction: any problems are highlighted early on. These considerations might lead to JCT MW11 as a suitable choice, but you might suggest that it is better to include the works in the main contract.
4. Begin to exclude particular contract types. This shows that you know about them and their appropriate use. For example, JCT MW11 or the Intermediate Building Contract (IC11) would not be appropriate for a single contract with a value of £3 million.
5. This leaves you with a number of options: JCT SBC11, and Design and Build forms, and possibly other forms, such as NEC3.

6. You should then discuss why you would choose one of these and the various options (With Sub-contractor's Design Agreement (SBCSU6/A), for example). Your recommendation should be informed by a number of factors: client attitude to risk, cost certainty, the likelihood of unforeseen events (this relates back to point 3) and possible design quality issues.
7. You might touch on tendering methods and lead-in times.
8. You might speculate about the 'one-off' nature of the project, how the procurement route might change if the project were one of a series of similar projects, and the nature of the specialist works.
9. Make a recommendation.

The scenario usually addresses a wide range of issues, including the architect's appointment, procurement and works on site.

ISSUE-BASED QUESTIONS

This last type of question is included because the scenario might be limited and cannot be 'stretched' to accommodate all the areas that need to be assessed. Such a question might take the form of a single contractual issue, a mini-scenario not related to the main scenario, possibly another project in the imaginary office concerning, as an example, defects. Alternatively it might not be scenario-based but rather address a wide range of issues, such as employment, partnering in construction, professional Codes and Standards.

To provide a satisfactory answer requires a mix of the techniques discussed above. You must show that you are aware of the key issues and then be able to discuss them more fully, giving examples to demonstrate your understanding and knowledge.

Putting these ideas into practice – some sample examination questions and answers

The following examples are based on real questions and real student answers from a range of Part 3 examinations. These samples have been provided to show how to approach the questions. They are not model answers. The commentary is intended to highlight good and bad points in examination technique and give you an idea of the level of detail required to answer a question successfully.

The first (Q.1) is a scenario-based question from a three-hour, time-limited 'open book' examination where you need to answer five questions. Approximately 35 minutes should be allowed to answer the question. This should allow some time to read the questions thoroughly, to plan your answer and to check your whole script at the end – and possibly to give you some time to complete an answer in case you go over your time target.

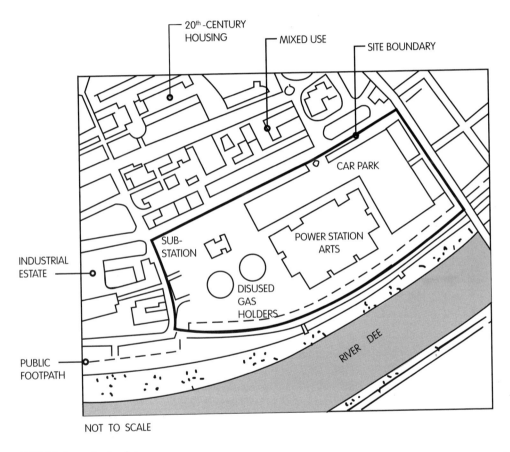

NOT TO SCALE

FIGURE 3.1 Scenario site plan

The general scenario explains that the student is working for a large architectural practice. The practice has been asked to act as architect for the conversion of a redundant gas works site into an art installation space linked to a Grade II 'listed' former power station which is now a successful contemporary art venue. The site is owned by the client – 'Powerstation Arts'.

The scenario plan is there to help you. Look at it carefully to establish the key concerns and also look at the context of the site and the adjoining properties. Look for clues about the setting: a river on one boundary; an industrial rather than a residential setting.

Is there a listing as well as a planning issue?

Do you think it is in a Conservation Area?

The gas storage tanks ('holders' or 'gasometers') indicate an industrial past and the likelihood of site contamination.

The change from redundant industrial to gallery and arts use should be noted.

The electrical sub-station means that the utilities are involved too.

Look at site access. How will it be affected by the project?

First, look for the operative work or phrase. This question is asking for a 'report format' answer. It can take the form of a set of short statements that address specific points. It is not asking for you to reach a conclusion – but other questions might. However, having set out the key issues you could comment on whether this proposed project is going to be contentious or difficult.

So there are two areas to be addressed: i) the statutory factors and legislation affecting the development; and ii) 'any other matters'. This would include common land law issues. You must address both aspects of the question for full marks.

Note: there are two activities here: i) referring to the legislation and ii) who you would consult. The objective is to show your knowledge and then to put it in context.

The objective here is to show both your understanding of the application of the legislation to the project and the practical effects. Therefore identify any delaying factors and the possible duration of the delay – delays caused by the planning process itself, for example. (There are published statutory timescales.)

So the question is in two parts. This is designed to help you and the script marker. Look for the value of each part and allocate time accordingly. The weighting indicates that Part a requires 50% more effort than Part b. However much you add to each section you will only get the maximum. Be careful also to answer both parts: a good answer to Part 1.a will only get you a maximum of 12/20. You might find that apportioning time will help; 14 minutes = 8 marks maximum. Do not be too formulaic though. In this question it gives you a clear indication also about the amount of information and level of detail required.

The scenario and the scenario plan are both there to guide you to the relevant areas being tested in the question and both provide material you can use. The question itself will also contain further information.

Questions are carefully written, so read them carefully too. The question writer has to tread a fine line between leading you to the issues and giving you the answer. Therefore look for key words in the questions. In Question 1, these include 'statutory' (it occurs twice – in Part 1.a and again in 1.b), and 'legislation'. You should, by now, know the subject area being tested. But also, look carefully for *how* you are expected to apply your knowledge. For example, explaining the organisations you should consult with is important.

When looking at the scenario plan, be systematic. Look out for the following:

> The site boundary and the relationship with adjoining buildings.
> The context of the site or building. Very often the site is in an urban setting. Other buildings may be indicated as important – a civic building, possibly with a date or period of construction.
> Surrounding uses.
> Rivers and waterways.
> Possible underground or above ground obstacles such as drains and power lines as well as possible rights of way.
> How you access the site.

EXAMPLE 1

Question 1

The office has been invited to a meeting with the client to discuss the potential for the site and any regulatory issues that may affect the scheme and the development programme.

Study the scenario plan and prepare a short report on the main statutory factors and any other matters that should be considered. Your answer should:

a) refer to the legislation, appropriate available relevant information and various organisations that you would consult with (12 marks); and

b) evaluate the likely effect that relevant statutory procedures will have on the early stages of the development programme (8 marks).

(20 marks in total)

Here is a sample framework of issues that need to be addressed:

Question 1.a

In this part of the question the examiner is looking for *major* factors.

Legislation:

Town and Country Planning

Reference points:
> Local Plan
> National Planning Policy Framework (NPPF)
  Consult:
  • Local authority development control
  • Planning consultant
  • Access consultant
> Section 106 Agreement(s) and Community Infrastructure Levy (CIL)
  Consult:
  • Local authority
  • Specialist and legal advisors

Conservation Area and Listed Building

Reference points:
> Local Plan
> NPPF
  Consult:
  • Local authority conservation officer
  • English Heritage
  • Specialist heritage architect
  • Planning consultant

Sustainability

Reference points:
> Flood risk data, transport studies
  Consult:
  • Environment Agency
  • Specialist consultant hydrologist
  • Transport consultant:

Health and Safety
Reference points:
> CDM Regulations
> Asbestos Regulations, etc.
  Consult:
  - Local authority Environmental Health Department
  - HSE
  - CDM co-ordinator

Highways
Reference points:
> Local Plan
> Central government guidelines
  Consult:
  - Local authority Highways Department
  - Consultant civil engineer

Party walls (if relevant)
Reference points:
> Party Wall, etc. Act 1996
  Consult:
  - Party wall surveyor
  - Adjoining owners

Adjoining owners' rights, and rights of others over site
Reference points:
> Land Registry data
> Deeds to site
  Consult:
  - Client solicitor
  - Utility companies
  - Specialist surveyor: rights to light

Question 1.b

This part of the question is asking for the likely effect of the **procedures** on the **early** stages of the development programme. This should lead you to RIBA Work Stages 0 and 1. Your task is to explain the activities and possible timescales to your client.

Planning
> Preparation of agreed design to brief
> Pre-application advice
> Consultation
> Preparation of specialist reports and surveys
> Application (including type of application and why): registration, public consultation, time for decision (varies)
> Decision
> Planning permission: 'reserved matters' to be addressed or 'conditions' to be met
> Refusal: appeal (but note the question does not expect you to give full details of appeal procedures)
> Section 106 Agreement: note time to negotiate and agree with specialists and possible effects on design
> Community Infrastructure Levy

Listed Buildings/ Conservation Area Consent
> Running in parallel to rather than following planning
> Possible problems of specialist consultation with English Heritage taking additional time – requests for further information and lack of clarity with the process

Sustainability
> Additional information: transport studies
> Flood Risk Assessment – hydrologist reports and negotiations with Environment Agency

Health and safety
> Note early contact with CDM-C
> Time for surveys
> Unforeseen risks

Highways
> Runs in parallel with Town Planning

Party walls
> Will not affect early stages but it is advantageous to start *statutory procedures* set out in the Party Wall, etc. Act 1996 and negotiations so as not to affect later stages of the project
> Note that separate consultation and negotiation with each adjoining owner affected by the works will take time

Adjoining owners
> Will not affect early stages but it will be advantageous to start negotiations so as not to affect later stages of the project

---

'Health warning'

The sample framework is not intended to be *comprehensive* or applicable to *all* questions of this type. It aims to show a simple, systematic approach to a complex scenario. Before attempting to answer any question, the following points are worth bearing in mind.

> Read the question *carefully*, to pick up *all* the points it asks you to address and to apply your *relevant* knowledge to the scenario.
> A 'scattergun' approach, where you set down everything you know regardless of its relevance, is unlikely to be successful. The examiner will be concerned about whether you *understand* what you show that you *know*. For example, this question asks for specific information at a particular stage in the project. The Building Regulations might be referred to but are not necessarily relevant to the early stages of the development or the procedures at that stage.
> Always relate your answers to the scenario.
> Show that your knowledge is current. The legislation referred to in this question changes continuously. For example, at the time of writing the planning legislation, in particular, is due for major changes.

Note that you must not rely on the accuracy of the technical content in the sample answers in this book. Planning policy and procedures, in particular, are subject to change. The central aim is to improve your exam technique, not to impart technical knowhow.

A good start but a better answer would include a summary of the key points that are going to be covered. This helps to order your thoughts and give a coherence to your answer.

Good – although the text could be more precise the answer addresses one key requirement – to look at the Local Plan. The student also shows an understanding of the role of central government through reference to the NPPF.

A better answer would refer to the elements of the NPPF that are relevant to the site and the project. This will be required when preparing the planning application.

Good – this is always a good starting point. The reference to objections shows an understanding of the process in practice.

Good – this shows a clear understanding of heritage and conservation legislation and how they work in practice.

A better answer would look at the site plan carefully and suggest that it is unlikely that it is a Conservation Area. This would show a better understanding of the legislation and its context.

The answer has now moved beyond Town Planning legislation to other statutory considerations.

This part of the answer is weaker but the student does pick up on environmental legislation.

The sample answers below are actual answers from recent examinations. They have been left in a relatively raw state, although note that small errors have been corrected.

Sample Answer A

The following is a brief report first considering wider issues and after looking at the context of the site.

a) First, we would need to consult the local planning authority website to ascertain the current Local Plan. This is a summary of the local authority's continuing objectives and policies for the area, and is required by the Town and Country Planning Acts. The Local Plan is also informed by the NPPF. These are available through the Planning Portal.

We would also carry out some 'desktop research' to investigate the planning history of the site, to ascertain whether any previous planning applications had been made, their outcome and any relevant objections that might have been made at the time.

Also, the local authority can inform us of any Enterprise Zones which allow for a less onerous process of planning submission.

The gas works might be 'listed'. If so English Heritage would need to be informed and consulted throughout the design phase, as required by the Listed Buildings and Conservation Areas Act 1990. Listed Building Consent is required for demolition, alterations and additions within the site. If the building is not 'listed' but falls within a conservation area, consent will also be required for demolition or partial demolition if required by the works. The application for demolition is now part of the planning application process.

Also, we would need to contact the Environment Agency regarding the redundant gas holders (tanks) and the local authority regarding likely contamination of the land. A desktop study of previous uses of the site will show the nature of the contamination, under the Contaminated Land Act 2000.

The site would be subject to a flood risk assessment under the Environment Act 1995.

67

This is the only part of the report that considers land law. Ideally the answer should be more specific. It does at least show some knowledge of the subject area – but not how to apply that knowledge.

Another relevant consideration. Access can be problematic – as can traffic. It may also be the subject of a Section 106 Agreement.

At first sight this looks like a fair opening statement but it is not supported by any facts. How useful is it? We do not get an idea of the actual timescales for the statutory procedures or potential problems that may be encountered. To be a useful report it should consider the time needed for preparing a planning application, including pre-application advice, and the time required for a decision. The same applies to other statutory applications.

It might be useful to state that this possible delay is unknown at this stage – hence the need to identify risks as soon as possible

This is good. It shows a recognition of the use of planning conditions and their effect on the programme.

A good point. There may be options other than restoration, such as relocation.

This would generally apply to public drainage only that cross the site.

It will be necessary to establish whether there are any easements and/or restrictive covenants. For example, there may electrical cables under the site. It would be necessary to liaise with the electrical supply company to establish what restrictions apply and any access requirements.

Lastly under the Highways Act 1980 it will be necessary to inform the Highways Agency of any proposed changes to access.

b) Many of the statutes outlined above will not seriously hinder the programme. However English Heritage may delay the design development if they are not happy with the effect on the Listed Building and its curtilage.

Contaminated land may delay early site construction work if it is more serious than indicated by the initial survey. The local authority may specify planning conditions demanding that contaminated land work is fully completed before the main work commences.

If bats and protected species are found they may delay construction until the Environment Agency is happy that their habitat is restored.

Upon excavation for construction unmapped drains and sewers may be discovered which would require notification to the local authority.

Summary comments on Sample Answer A

This answer demonstrates that the candidate has a reasonably good knowledge of the essential legislation and answers the question in a short report format.

In the answer to 1a it does this by providing a clear structure and referring to the relevant legislation very effectively and succinctly at each point in the report. It covers key issues and keeps it relevant to the scenario by providing relevant examples.

The answer to 1b makes a simple statement about the effect on the development and then goes on to set out briefly the reasons why. This part of the question lacks detail, though, and does not follow through with any real information on the procedures discussed in 1.a. 'Many of the statutes…' is too vague and there is no reference to the planning process itself – which is central to the question. Other than 'notification', there is little to say about the 'procedures' referred to in the question. This suggests that the knowledge is adequate but that an understanding of how to apply that knowledge is limited.

This sets the scene reasonably well. The most valuable points are that the student realises that the project will have 'considerable public interest' and has a redundant industrial use plus the added complication of the sub-station. A better answer would set out more of the key issues. A valid criticism would be that nothing new has been added (other than the public interest issue) and that the student is 'feeding back' information already given in the question – not a good way to gain marks – and a waste of valuable time for both student and marker.

This is better. The student gets straight to the main planning issues and covers the listed building problem. The prospect of prosecution is also a good point – telling the client that all work must be authorised and approved.

A better answer would also refer to the NPPF and include a short statement about Conservation Area Consent and the likelihood or otherwise of it being in a Conservation Area.

Two good points here. However a better answer would separate the two – pre-application actions and 'major project' – but under examination conditions this is acceptable. Examiners will make some concessions for the lack of time available to order your thoughts. (Another good reason for thorough preparation.) Also, having shown that s/he knows that this is a major project, a reference to the different timescales for a decision to be given would be valuable advice to a client. A reference to public consultation would be appropriate here.

Good – a recognition that a Change of Use is required and the Use Classes is a bonus – again showing a deeper knowledge. Also, this is a good example of using standard references – it is very unlikely that s/he knows the Use Classes but was able to find them in the relevant text and then apply them to the scenario – an excellent technique. A very good answer would also refer to the need for a Design and Access Statement and the 'Sequential Test' required by the NPPF.

Here, s/he is beginning to address 'any other matters' – in this case contamination. Good referencing and then the application in the form of examples of the different surveys required. This comment would be improved by a short reference to the potential for delay to the programme.

This is acceptable under the time constraints but a better answer would refer to the legal procedures and the need for agreement to any proposals following consultation – this takes time – sometimes longer than the consultation itself.

Sample Answer B (to the same question)

This is a very large site. The site is bounded on three sides by what appear to be public roads and a river on the fourth side. Given the nature and use of the building this will be a high-profile project with considerable public interest. The newly-acquired land contains redundant industrial structures and buildings as well as an electrical substation.

Key development drivers

The Local Plan should be referred to in order to establish planning policy regarding development in this area. Early consultation with the planning authority is recommended to establish their views. Given the Grade II listing of the main building any work done on the site or to the existing building will require Listed Building Consent with likely additional requirements stipulating a required level of detail. No works, demolition or otherwise, can be commenced without consent. (If commenced without consent criminal prosecution is possible.)

As the scheme is likely to qualify as a 'major project' for the purposes of the planning application, pre-application advice/meetings would be sensible to reduce risk down the line.

There will also be a change of use for the new part of the site from B2 'General Industrial' to D2 'Assembly and Leisure'.

With a redundant gas works on the site there is likely to be contamination. The client should be aware of their duties in relation to the Environment Protection Act 1990. Possible ground/earth surveys, asbestos surveys will need to be undertaken.

Statutory undertakers/utilities companies should be consulted to establish any easements or wayleaves on the land especially in connection with the electrical substation on the site.

Here basic common land law issues are raised – but applied to the scenario.

This is a useful statement – only if it is relevant. It shows that s/he knows that party wall legislation may be an issue generally and then suggests that it would not be relevant in this particular scenario and gives a few simple reasons. As a rule, though, only refer to those matters that are directly pertinent – otherwise you may lose valuable time in the exam referring to matters that are not important.

Good – but a better answer would have linked CDM with the contamination issue previously highlighted. Also, s/he misses a key point that CDM will apply from the beginning of the project and site investigations in particular, given the contamination issue.

Good use of bullet points. They separate the different points clearly.

Good. This alerts the client to the need for pre-application advice and the possibility of a public consultation exercise.

Two separate points have been combined here. A better answer would distinguish between the planning timescales – including the timescale for a 'major project' (13 or 16 weeks rather than the normal 8 weeks) – and the utilities problem. However, this is forgiveable under examination conditions.

Good – a bonus piece of information – the possibility of a refusal and the options available.

The title deeds should be checked to confirm and establish boundaries, easements, rights of way and restrictive covenants that may burden the land.

Party wall issues do not appear to be relevant as there do not appear to be any adjoining buildings or structures in close proximity to the site boundary.

The CDM 2007 Regulations will play a key role in ensuring health and safety throughout the construction and future maintenance of the project. The client should be made aware of their CDM duties.

A full Building Regulations application will be required under The Building Act 1984 and the Regulatory Reform Order 2005 regarding fire regulations.

The Highways Act may also be relevant concerning changes to the access to the site.

b) Statutory procedures affecting the programme

> Pre-application advice: no definitive time lines. Generally takes about a month to set a meeting date. (It may be advisable to carry out public consultation prior to the planning submission. This will take time to prepare, notification is required and the consultation will also take a set, reasonable period.)
> Planning Application and Listed Building Consent and Conservation Area Consent (if required). The guidelines for these are 8 weeks for a decision. However if contentious, or if strong public objections are made this could increase. Statutory undertakers/utilities: if works to utilities (i.e. moving a water main, gas pipe or the electrical substation) are required the time involved is down to each company – this can drag on and typically be costly.
> If the planning application is refused an appeal can be made or a revised application can be submitted within 12 months at no extra charge.
> Appeal procedure: 3 methods: written submissions, informal hearing or public enquiry.) Time: 3–6 months from time appeal is made.

Which sample answer is the best?

Examiners are assessing three characteristics:

1. The depth and breadth of your knowledge.
2. The way you apply that knowledge in a professional context, which in this case is the scenario.

3. The way you structure your answer. The structure shows not only what you know but reflects how you order your thoughts to arrive at a (hopefully) coherent and in this case report-type answer.

The better your knowledge and your understanding of how to apply it, the better able you will be to work with similar issues as a professional architect.

Although there are gaps in both answers, particularly the second part of the question, Sample B is the better answer. Why? The level of knowledge and especially how it is applied is better. Each subject is more or less dealt with separately, making the information easier to absorb. Lastly, the way the information is structured is more coherent, indicating a better mastery of the subject material.

Remember also that examiners will generally work to an agreed plan so that they remain consistent across all the answers they mark. Papers will be sample second-marked and subject to institutional quality assurance procedures too.

Tips to improve the answer

Here are some points that would make for a better answer.

> Start with a clear, short introduction drawn from the scenario and setting out the key issues and content. In this scenario the following are important:
>   o This is a large prestigious public development project requiring planning permission and will require extensive consultation
>   o The existing redundant industrial use means a change of use
>   o The Listed Building requires further consideration
>   o The possibility of it being a Conservation Area needs investigating
>   o The site: The river should alert you to environmental factors such as flooding
>   o Contaminated land has health and safety implications from the outset
>   o Rights of way in connection with public utilities should be investigated
>   o Site access is currently restricted and should be investigated

Dealing with Question 1.a
> Relate these issues to the RIBA Plan of Work to place each issue in context and to focus on specific topics. Each point can then be dealt with in as much detail as possible given the time constraints. For example:

At Work Stages 0 and 1
The project requires planning consent under the Town and Country Planning Acts and so we will:
- Discuss proposals in principle with local planning authority.
- Investigate the planning history (any previous applications, consents or refusals, comments from the public, etc.).
- Study the NPPF and explain that this overrides the planning history.
- Investigate Listed Building and Conservation Area implications. If Listed or in a Conservation Area, Listed Building/Conservation Area Consent might be required under the Planning (Listed Buildings and Conservation Areas) Act 1990.
- Advise client to appoint a CDM Co-ordinator as required by the CDM Regulations, and carry out risk assessment of site prior to soil surveys for contamination (and notify project staff of risks) etc. Note that the headline legislation is the Health and Safety at Work Act 1974.
- Review the implications of river frontage and the possible need for flood prevention measures.
- Investigate rights of way and any restrictive covenants.
- Consult with statutory undertakers/utilities in connection with the existing electrical substation.
- Consider possible new access and consult with Highways Authority.
- Investigate any other policy matters that may have an impact on the site.

At Work Stages 2 and 3
- Obtain pre-application advice on proposals from planning authority for planning application.
- Carry out public consultation with a local design panel and the national body responsible for design standards, if relevant.
- Prepare a detailed planning application for the change of use and the new development work.
- Carry out an Environmental Impact Assessment to include any proposed flood prevention or mitigation measures.
- Prepare a Design and Access Statement including a sequential test as part of the planning application. This is because the development will be a public building and so the provisions of the Equality Act 2010 must be met. An access consultant might be employed to deal with this aspect of the project.

Work Stages 2 and 3

We will:

- Ensure that the project complies with the Building Regulations (Building Act 1984).
- Consult with the local building control department and either make a Full Plans application for their approval or appoint (under Sec.17) an approved advisor to give a certificate of compliance with the Building Regulations.
- Because it is a public building, ensure the project complies with the Fire Precautions Act 1971 and the subsequent Fire (Regulatory Reform) Order 2005 ('Fire Safety Order').
- Discuss its fire strategy with the fire authority.
- Along with the client, ensure that health and safety issues are assessed throughout all work stages as required by the CDM Regulations 2007.

Dealing with Question 1.b

> As a complex public building, the process of consultation and the formal applications that are required will take considerable time and the following should be factored into the design development programme:
  - Preliminary investigations and pre-application advice
  - Public consultation
  - Preparing the planning application
  - Processing the application
  - Normal application period
  - Major project application period (13 weeks)
> As the project is significant, it is likely that a Section 106 Agreement (TCPA 1990) will be required. This will involve considerable negotiation over the social betterment provisions that the local authority will require as a result of approving the proposals; the CIL will also be relevant.
> All of these will affect the design and construction programme. The planning consent will also have conditions that may need to be discharged before building works can start on site. This work could be extensive. For example, it might include flood prevention measures.
> Negotiations with the utility companies, if carried out promptly, may run concurrently and not affect the overall programme. Similarly, the routine applications for Building Regulations permission can normally be accommodated during the design programme. However, unusual aspects such as a novel fire strategy might require separate testing and approval, which of course will take extra time.

These tips do not amount to a conclusive or comprehensive answer, and took considerably longer than 35 minutes to prepare. It is therefore not a 'model answer'. The references to the later RIBA Work Stages will need to be justified and are, arguably, not relevant to the second part of the question.

Always demonstrate that you can think beyond the basic information required by the question. The reference to Section 106 of the Town & Country Planning Act 1990, linking town planning issues with the context and the programme, does just that. You should take the opportunity to show this deeper knowledge – but only where relevant.

The layout should give you a better idea of the different formats that can work effectively. Because the question does not ask you to discuss pros and cons, a bullet point format works well. Note that 1.a is not a list – each bullet point leads to a short statement. 1.b could also be more discursive but you are likely repeat yourself. Therefore the bullet points act as points of reference and also demonstrate your level of knowledge and understanding.

EXAMPLE 2

The next example is of a question that does not have a 'right' answer but a range of answers. So what are examiners looking for? As well as your knowledge and understanding of the relevant subject areas of the Part 3 Criteria, they are also assessing your powers of reasoning. They are looking for how you use the information you are given in the scenario and how you weigh it up to arrive at a recommendation. They will want to see that you have a solid rationale for selecting some options in favour of others. In the following example, the topics are procurement and contracts. It draws on some standard knowledge of different procurement options and then asks students to make a case-specific recommendation based on the scenario.

The two sample answers show two different approaches. Both are legitimate because they show a good depth and breadth of knowledge and the students their ability to apply their knowledge to the scenario.

By all means start with some clear notes. These are clearly here to help the student not the examiner but provided you do not put a line through them they will be read and assessed – possibly valuable if you are running out of time.

Question 2

(This follows on from Question 1. The budget is in excess of £50 million.)

With planning permission arriving a few days ago, the client wants to start construction in four months' time as key milestones must be reached in order for the staged funding for the project to be released. However, the client wants to retain a degree of design flexibility while the construction contract is running. Your office was instructed to start the detailed design of the more demanding design features of the project including the specialist brick cladding, three months ago, anticipating a positive decision from the local authority.

a) Evaluate the different procurement routes for the project (12 marks); and
b) discuss the most appropriate building contract (8 marks).

(20 marks in total)

Sample Answer C

Again, this is an actual real example, with a similar suggested time allocation of 35 minutes.

This example is much longer than normal and – unbelievably – was completed in around 35–40 minutes. Good answers need not be this long. As a general point, much of the early part falls into the 'textbook' category, where information is set out without much reference to the context. At worst it might not be relevant as most of the information is generic. It is only towards the end that the information is pulled together and contextualised. This answer could be much shorter and still retain its content and quality.

Notes:
Important elements for the client:
> Speed to enable funding release
> Design quality
> Flexibility during process

Possible procurement routes:
> Traditional (general contracting)
> Design and build
> Management contracting
> Construction management

A short introduction setting out the key issues would help to focus the discussion and shorten the explanations that follow.

What does follow is a reasonable explanation of the four main types of procurement. They provide a good description generally – although some points become 'bundled together' (the reference to Guaranteed Maximum Price, for example, is not exclusive to Design and Build Contracts.

A much better answer would relate the different methods to the scenario and discuss where they are appropriate.

This is a good point about novation and shows that the student has a very good depth as well as breadth of knowledge and understanding. This adds a level of detail that sets it above the normal. An exceptional answer would contextualise this further – 'Would novation be appropriate?' – If not, why not?

a)

Traditional (general contracting)
Powerstation Arts would appoint a design team and commission them to produce design and contract documentation. They would then select a contractor by competitive tendering or negotiation and this contractor would agree to complete the construction to the contract documents for a contract sum. The client would appoint a contract administrator to act in their interests during the construction stage and oversee the contract implementation and price the interim certificates (the consideration for performance).

Design and Build (D&B)
Powerstation Arts would appoint a contactor to 'design and build' the facility. As the design team has already been appointed and started design work, the most appropriate form of design and build contract would be one that novated the current team to the contractor once the Employer's Requirements have been produced and the contract formalised. The contractor would be issued with the Employer's Requirements (and could include a performance specification) and from these documents would produce his Contractor's Proposals. Powerstation Arts would then need to check the proposals for deviations from the Employer's Requirements. The contractor would then agree to complete the works for a contract sum (and possibly a guaranteed maximum price). The client would be able to appoint an Employer's Agent to give advice during the contract and construction stages but if we were novated to the contractor we would not be able to take this role due to the clash of interests as the contractor would now be our client and employer. We would be therefore unable to act for both contractor and Powerstation Arts.

Management Contracting
The client would appoint a management contractor alongside the design team. The management contractor would then appoint all necessary works contractors for the construction phase. He would split the works into packages and let the contracts separately and sequentially in line with the construction programme.

By the end of this part of the question the examiner has a good sense that the student has a better-than-average knowledge and understanding of procurement generally. You will see that some of the summaries are fairly short but are more than adequate.

This is satisfactory although there is some vagueness about the benefits of this type of procurement. The comment regarding cost certainty could be challenged as lack of certainty is commonly one of the reasons GC is not used.

This is a bold – and not entirely correct – assertion. GC is not seen as assuring cost certainty as the contract traditionally allows for variations to be made with relative ease when compared with design and build contracts. There is scope for argument if variations are not covered by the schedules of rates in the tender documents.

This is a little confused. A better answer would start with the part about the early start on site and explain why. The point about Design and Build not accommodating change easily is a good one – however s/he needs to explain why this is important or relevant.

Construction Management

Powerstation Arts would appoint the design team and also appoint a construction manager to organise both the design team and the construction phases of the project. The Construction Manager would split up the works and the packages would be tendered and let separately and sequentially as per management contracting above. The difference being that Powerstation Arts would appoint all the trade contractors giving them direct contractual links with all parties of the project.

b)

General Contracting (GC) would allow the client flexibility whilst the construction contract is running via the variation and instruction mechanisms within the project. The contract would also allow cost certainty once the tenders had been returned and the means to price variations to the contract in line with the tendered contract documents. It would allow the employer an active involvement in the project and design quality would be unlikely to suffer as the design team would be maintained throughout the construction phase. GC also allows for the incorporation of complexity in the project which is stated as being required.

Design and Build (D&B) would not be the most suitable form as it has the least capacity to incorporate client changes once the contractor's proposals have been finalised and agreed. It would allow an early start on site and a single point for any liability issues as the contractor would have complete responsibility for both the design and construction of the works. It is also perhaps not the best suited for a complex high interest project such as the gallery as it may not be possible to maintain design quality, depending on how advanced the design drawings and specifications were at the tender stage.

Management Contracting (MC) would not have a fixed contract value and this would mean the client would be unsure of the final contract sum until nearing completion as all the packages are tendered separately and sequentially. MC would allow an early start on site but at the expense of cost certainty.

As with the earlier section on GC, there is some confusion of independent points. There is a sense that cost certainty is important. However, the student could have said that there are ways to reduce the risk to the budget by having either a guaranteed maximum price (common in this type of procurement for this reason) and a robust cost plan that is effectively managed.

In practice it is very unlikely that this project would go down the general contracting route. It is very large and complex and it would be very difficult to prepare the necessary contract documentation in the funding timescales. However, the student goes on to give a reasoned and reasonable justification for this procurement route.

This is the best part of the answer. The student draws the issues together and explains why s/he considers that GC is the best procurement method.

The contract choice adds to the display of knowledge and the points about Specialist Contractor Design (SCD) portions show a deeper understanding of the design challenges and complexities of the project.

The final comments about an enabling contract will earn bonus points.

Construction Management. As with MC above, construction management would not provide any cost certainty at the outset and with funding not fully secured I think this would be unwise as a procurement route. The client does not appear from the scenario to be a risk taker and this is a large-scale, complex project that would be very public during its construction. There would be a great emphasis perhaps on quality at the expense of a fast finish to the project. CM would allow an early start on site and would cope with the complexity but in balancing the requirements I think General Contracting would be a better option.

Why General Contracting?

The architects are experienced in large scale projects (Note: this information is given in the scenario) so would be able to resource the management of a large scheme such as the Powerstation Arts gallery. The client needs to be relatively certain of costs and is obviously after a high quality, well-detailed end product. General contracting would allow this because of the involvement of the design team through construction and familiar, understood contractual principles.

I would suggest the innovative cladding system *(given in the scenario)* was included in the contract particulars as a Sub-contractor Design Agreements & Conditions so access to the contractor's specialists was available early on in the process for best integration of design intent, fabrication and finished appearance.

Allowing the specialist sections of work to be SCD items aligns design and fabrication in a single process because the contractor would develop the design proposals. It would also aid the design team with completing the other areas of the project.

JCT SBC 11 with Quantities with SCDs is a widely used form of contract that has been tested in the courts. For this and other stated reasons I consider that it would be a sensible choice for such a high-profile project. Risk has been apportioned fairly to all parties and, if well managed, will give the client a balance between cost certainty and design quality.

To enable an early start on site I would recommend a separate enabling works contract to be let between the parties. This would also allow site conditions to be assessed more thoroughly.

This introductory paragraph immediately sets out the key issues that will affect procurement and rightly recognises that the experience of the client and the established relationships and expertise are important.

A better answer might raise the client's attitude to risk – as a public sector client they are risk-averse even if this is partly offset by their experience of large projects.

This is a good approach. The student recognises the value and characteristics of general contracting – in this case the need to produce all the information at the tender stage – as the way to control the risk of cost and time overruns. This is then dismissed as impractical on a project of this complexity coupled with the funding deadline.

S/he raises the key point: the design development risk.

A better answer would briefly discuss how this could be resolved: two-stage tendering, novation of the design team as a way of retaining and developing the design intent.

This is a clear explanation of the advantages of management contracting and why it is appropriate to this project. However, stylistically, the sentences are over-long. They would benefit from being shorter – one point per sentence.

Sample Answer D

Again a real answer.

a)

It appears from the scenario that, for this particular client, funding deadlines and the need for a high quality design outcome are the most important aspects of the project. They have had previous experience working with the architect and the fact that they continue to work with them suggests a degree of trust has been built between them. The client is likely to have a high level of knowledge and expertise in the sector and is therefore open to a higher level of risk. The size of the project is also an important factor. At £50 million, this is a substantial investment by the client.

It is unlikely that this job would be procured under a traditional contract due to the scale of the project and the fact that there are imminent funding deadlines for which it would be unlikely to have a fully complete design package ready before, despite the early start by the design team. Traditional procurement would however allow a degree of flexibility in the contract to allow the employer to vary the design as the project develops and to a relatively advanced stage. (This may have an adverse effect on the timescale leading up to tendering, though.)

I would suggest that design and build would be an unlikely choice because although it may offer the benefits of an early start on site to meet funding deadlines, it would not allow any flexibility in the design development as the contractor's proposals would form the basis of the contract.

I would suggest that the most appropriate procurement route in this case would be management contracting. This is for several reasons. First, it would enable an early start on site to meet funding deadlines as I would anticipate the architects, having started work, would be able to provide sufficient information to tender for the early works. It will enable the architects to develop designs for the key aspects – including the specialist cladding – with specialist subcontractors at an early stage because in management contracting all the works contractors are employed directly by the management contractor.

Other benefits of management contracting in this case would include the ability to develop and modify the design requirements during construction and the benefits this would bring in terms of quality.

The comments about risk help to resolve the issues, as do those about the team and tendering. A criticism would be that s/he combines two different points: the experience of the team and competitive tendering. This confuses rather than clarifies – but is acceptable under examination conditions.

This paragraph has been left as written as an example of bad technique in an otherwise very well-written answer. The sentences are hopelessly over-long and difficult to read. Again, the student has combined two completely different points. The plus point is that they are mentioned but the negative point is that it is confusing and leaves the examiner possibly wondering if the student understands what they have written. In this case – on balance – they probably do. Some simple re-drafting or simply splitting up the paragraph into shorter sentences that separate out the points would significantly improve the answer. This can be done quickly if you allow sufficient time for checking at the end of the paper – without changing the content.

Avoid this type of speculation. The plus point is that it shows that the student knows about bespoke agreements but the negative point – a subtle one – is that it arguably undermines the reasons given for using a Standard Form. On balance it is acceptable but only because of the content. It narrowly risked being consigned to 'waffle'.

The risk would mainly lie with the client. However, as suggested previously, the client's experience on early substantial projects and our office's skills should allow a degree of trust to be built and to create an efficient team. This solution also maintains a degree of competitive tendering for the works packages and therefore the best cost can be achieved for specific parts including the more specialist items.

b)

The contractual relationship in a management contract is between the client and the management contractor, with all the subcontractors and works contractors employed directly by the management contractor. In this respect the management contractor is the single point of control for the project but due to fluctuations in cost and design that are allowed or may be required and the previous experience of the parties involved it is quite likely that the client would have developed their own bespoke agreement for a project of this kind with collateral warranties obtained by the client for the work of subcontractors/works contractors as otherwise no direct contractual agreement would exist in this method of procurement.

Re-drafted paragraph:
Here's how the last paragraph could have been redrafted for greater clarity.

The contractual relationship in a management contract is between the client and the management contractor. All the sub-contractors and works contractors are employed directly by the management contractor, making the management contractor the single point of control. As there is no direct contractual agreement between contractor and sub-contractor in this method of procurement, the client should obtain collateral warranties with the sub-contractors and works contractors.

Design development and cost fluctuations can be accommodated more easily than in a design and build contract. However, the potential for change will need effective control by the design team and a robust, realistic cost plan. The experience of the client and the competence of the design team in managing the previous project means that they are more likely to effectively control these risks.

S/he concludes with a choice of contract but gives us some further details of the contract and their relevance to the project.

Bringing the discussion to a close by referring back to the masterplan and the possibility of phased completion shows a very good breadth and depth of knowledge and understanding.

I would however recommend that a standard form of contract be used for the project. The JCT MC11 is specifically designed for management contracting and means that all the clauses are designed to work together. It also has associated documents that can help govern the agreements with works contractors. The standard form will allow options to deal with retention, variations, payment and dispute resolution, and make these clear. It also helps to spread risk more evenly as a bespoke contract may be set up to be biased towards the organisation that produced it. Supplements for phased completion can also be used should this be a desirable option and which may be useful in implementing the masterplan for the project.

Which sample answer is the best?

Both take very different approaches to the question and arrive at different conclusions, so it is difficult to separate them. Answer C is set out like a textbook, following the format of any of the standard works. The first part of the question (a) would be much better if it contextualised the knowledge by applying it more effectively to the scenario. Also, there is a sense that the student does not fully understand the detail of the general contracting method and this is the weakest part of the answer. (It is therefore perhaps risky later in the answer to suggest that this is the most appropriate procurement option.) There is a lot of content, though. The point about novation in design and build contracts is well made. The approach, though, runs the risk of repetition later in the question. Without sufficient context the examiner is left wondering if the student understands the knowledge s/he has acquired. But at least the information is there – it just needs to be applied better.

Part (b) is much better and builds on the main points. The assertion about 'cost certainty' is unusual – most commentators would disagree. Also the assertion is confused with a point about key rates being agreed at the tender stage.

The student's mistake has been retained in this book to show that we all make mistakes or have strong and weak points. To have sanitised the answer would give you an unrealistic idea of what a good 'real' answer looks like.

A Professional Examiner reviewing this student's work might decide that this is a point for discussion at the oral examination – not to challenge the student's statement as being wrong but to ask how and why they make that conclusion.

The section on design and build is the strongest. Good points are made about management contracting and construction management, but they are not developed – and repeat the phrase 'separately and sequentially' without really explaining what it means.

The last paragraph headed 'Why General Contracting?' brings the answer up to a much better standard. We get new, relevant information and a demonstration of a deeper understanding of the contract form (rather than the method of procurement). The reference to an enabling contract shows a better understanding of the problems raised by the project than the earlier part. Without this late surge of information and some limited discussion, the answer would have been so-so rather than good. For the purposes of the examination the student has shown a generally thorough approach to the process which compensates for the rather unlikely choice of General Contracting as the preferred route. Imagine, though, if they had selected this route without any analysis – that would raise serious concerns.

From the beginning Answer D is a discussion of the features of different procurement routes and their suitability for this project. The student takes account of the client's attitude to risk and the scale of the project. These comments, together with those about the strengths of the project team, show a good understanding of the context of the project. The student immediately applies his/her knowledge to the scenario, setting up the potential for deeper analysis than is possible with the 'textbook' approach adopted by the writer of Answer C.

The answer does not, however, display the breadth of knowledge of Answer C. For example, tendering is not mentioned, neither is the possibility of novating the design team to the contractor. The answer does not mention other mechanisms such as a separate enabling contract. Also, towards the end there is some confusion of ideas. We do get more detail on the way the contract could be administered – and its relevance to the project. However, if there was more content then it had the potential to be an excellent answer.

It should be stressed that there is more information that could be added and there are some evident gaps in knowledge shown. However, the answers should give you a flavour of the different possible approaches and what students can really achieve under time-limited conditions. Perhaps they will also help you decide which approach suits you best and the level of knowledge and understanding expected of you.

The next type of question is from an office-based examination where students are given more. As a result the questions can be more realistic – but also more complex. This next question asks for a letter.

EXAMPLE 3

Question 3

This question is taken from an unseen, 'open book', time-limited examination where ten questions are answered over a two-day period in the workplace – five questions a day. This allows approximately 1½ hours per question rather than the 35 minutes recommended for the earlier questions. Students cannot consult colleagues but they can consult other sources of information. Just as the questions are longer and more complex, so the expectation is that the answers will be too.

Scenario:

At the last site meeting on the project it was clear that the contractor had fallen behind with the contract works. You have now received a letter from the contractor. The office is administering the contract under a standard form of contract: JCT SBC05.

FAO Michael Bunney
Jade and Small Architects
Fallow Way
Elton,
HP44 3ND

7th March 2014

Dear Sirs,

GK Pharmaceuticals – extension to HQ Building

Under the terms of the above contract we hereby give notice that the progress of the work has been delayed.

The specific matters that have led to this delay are as follows:

1. Very bad and unexpected weather conditions over the early winter period.
2. Delay in the release and receipt of the door schedule. This was some three weeks later than set out in the information release schedule.
3. An extended delivery period on the 'plasticrete' specialist resin flooring specified in the contract documents which has delayed the installation by our sub-contractor.

We now estimate that the combined and projected effect of the above events has led to an overall delay to the construction programme of eight weeks.

Yours faithfully

Joseph Broadbent
Director
TK Construction PLC

Question

1. Prepare a memorandum to the director-in-charge explaining how you have assessed the claim for the extension of time and any entitlement to loss and expense; and
2. Draft a letter to the contractor giving your decision.

The question therefore has two parts. First, the memorandum – which allows you to show your understanding of the contract issues and the contractual procedures; and second, a letter – to show that you can write a short, formal letter giving your interim decision on a contractual claim.

It is very unlikely that you will have had experience of handling a claim of this kind, let alone making a decision and writing a formal letter to the contractor. Don't worry! Remember that the Part 3 Criteria do not require experience of every aspect of architectural practice. But you do need to demonstrate that you can use your knowledge of the standard form contract conditions and, as contract administrator, make an impartial decision regarding a contractual claim based on the available facts. The requirement for a letter is to show that you can communicate in the appropriate manner, or 'register', in this case a formal reply to the contractor. Effective communication and presentation are both Part 3 Criteria that reflect your professionalism as well as your knowledge.

The starting point is to refer back to the relevant condition in the JCT SBC11 contract. The contractor's letter is making a claim for an extension of time. The relevant section of the contract is Clause 2 and its sub-clauses.

The examination is not the appropriate time to start acquainting yourself with the contract. You should, through lectures that guide you through the contract and in personal study, have familiarised yourself with a standard form of contract. You will be expected to understand the role of the architect as contract administrator even if all your experience has, for example, been on design and build projects.

Full address, any reference and date are missing, which is unprofessional.

This is a formal contractual letter. As it is a request by the contracting company, 'Dear Sirs' would be a more appropriate start. If the letter had been to an individual then a personal reply might be appropriate, but in the form 'Dear Mr Broadbent'

The full project title is needed.

The register and tone of the letter are completely inappropriate. This informality is unacceptable.

Again, this is completely inappropriate. The architect is acting as an impartial judge of the merits of the contractor's claim. This is far too partisan and informal.

This is not the time for excuses. Still woefully informal.

The candidate is wrong here – the sub-contractor's performance is the contractor's responsibility, as is the timely supply of materials.

The architect is inviting the contractor to claim additional costs. Wrong! Any claim should be assessed against the terms of the contract.

Sample Answer E

Again based on a real answer.

1. Letter to contractor

Jo Broadbent
TK Construction plc

Dear Jo,

GK Pharma: HQ Extension project

Thanks for your letter about the problems you have been having on the GK Pharma job. I have had a look at the reasons for the delay and I have some good news.

Congratulations!

I agree with you about the bad weather in December – it really was cold!

Also, I am really sorry about the delay in issuing the hardware schedule. I wish you had told us earlier and I would have tried to do something about it. I did have a hunch that it might cause a problem but I forgot to talk to you about it.

I checked out the problem with the Plasticrete resin floor. I called the supplier and he told me that as they were snowed under with orders. He tried to speak to John Howe on site but he was on holiday in France so he sent the stuff allocated to our project somewhere else. He told me it happened all the time. I can see that this was out of your hands.

So the eight weeks are yours. Can you give me an idea on any extra costs so that I can pass these on to the QS.

I hope that this is ok.

Regards

Mike

Commentary on Answer E

Unbelievably, this example is based on a recent real examination answer. There are a number of issues that you should be aware of. From an examiner's viewpoint – and a professional one concerning day-to-day professional practice – these fall into the following categories:

1. Presentation: 'Is the 'tone' of the letter appropriate?'
2. Content and factual accuracy: 'Does the writer show sufficient knowledge and understanding of the issues?'

Presentation and exam technique

Presentation is more than how something looks – although that is understandably important in a design practice. It goes to the heart of how we present and conduct ourselves generally as professionals. Under the Part 3 Criteria there is a whole section on Professionalism. In this context the question is testing the candidate's ability to present information to a senior colleague and to give them advice they can rely on and also address the client in the appropriate manner. Linguists call this appropriate manner the appropriate 'register'.

Register is important because we use it all the time – so much so that we are barely aware of it. It is the style of language adopted to communicate with different groups of people in different circumstances. There are many different registers on a scale from the very formal, such as making a speech in a court of law, to very relaxed and informal, such as when talking amongst friends, family or children. Generally, we adjust our register instinctively. It affects the way we write, the way sentences are constructed, the precision with which we use words or phrases and even grammar and punctuation.

In a professional context you should consider every communication as meeting certain standards from polite and considerate to accurate and factual. Every email – and even every phone conversation – could be used in a wider arena if there was a legal dispute.

Emails present a particular problem because, unlike letters, they are instant. We press 'send' before checking them and they fly off to the wrong inbox causing offence and escalating disagreements in a way impossible to have imagined. Take great care.

The Freedom of Information Act might also affect you if you are working in or for the public sector. If a dispute goes to court then it takes place in the public view. This applies equally to a disciplinary hearing by the ARB.

Register is important because you will be called upon to write formal contractual letters – for example, to confirm appointment terms or to resolve a contractual claim or to agree the new appointment of a member of staff. Your professional business and your future employees will be relying upon your ability to communicate accurately and professionally. Also, in the context of your wider professional duties, clients, contractors and other members of the design team are going to rely on your professionalism. If you are leading the design team then it is incumbent on you to set the right standards.

It need hardly be said that Answer E strikes completely the wrong register for a formal letter to a contractor which sets out the territory for resolving a contractual claim. There is also a more serious knock-on effect. The colloquial tone suggests a lack of proper professional independence, as required under the contract. The employer might think you are siding with the contractor whereas your duty is to make an impartial judgement of the claim from the contractor. You also owe a duty under the terms of your appointment to your client to act with reasonable skill and care. On this count alone the letter fails because it is clearly unprofessional.

To find good examples, look through the files available to you at work. These may be letters from other consultants, such as solicitors and cost consultants who are used to writing dry, accurate contractual letters. Refer to one of the publications that contain some examples of 'standard' letters such as the *Architect's Handbook of Practice Management*.[4] If in doubt, exaggerate the formality. No one will criticise you for being too formal, especially at Part 3.

Content and factual accuracy

The letter also fails on the second count: content and factual accuracy. The writer does not show us that they understand the issues or how to address them. Some issues have been ignored and others have been dealt with incorrectly. The memo that the question also asks for should demonstrate your knowledge and understanding by setting out a decision-making process. It may reach the 'wrong' conclusion but examiners will be looking for your approach to the problem, the way you use sources and references, your understanding of them as much as the conclusions you reach.

How much to demonstrate in the answer

Examiners know that there's a limit to how much you can do in the time available to you. They will make concessions but will, however, want to see that you respond in a professional manner and that all the principal issues are dealt with thoughtfully and with reasonable care. They will, as mentioned before, be guided by advice from the examining organisation, which will have carefully drafted and redrafted the questions to ensure that the appropriate level of information can be delivered in the time available.

You should be familiar with the JCT SBC11 contract clauses and have carefully considered how you are going to use the contract *before* the examination. At least have a mental picture of what the key clauses are, where they are and what they are used for. A time-limited examination is the last place to be searching for the relevant subjects in the contract. The good news is that most construction contracts, although long and complicated, nevertheless follow a similar format and address similar issues. With practice you can find your way around the clauses fairly quickly. You are unlikely to pick up this skill through experience in architectural practice so study is the key, coupled with working through past papers.

This is a much better answer. First, we have a recognisable letter format.

Good – a clear summary of the key issues. This is a case where briefly repeating the information in the question helps to frame the answer. Although no marks will be given for this repetition it summarises the problem and gives the examiner some confidence that the student understands the key issues.

In practice the contractor does not need to be told this but it shows the examiner that the student is aware of the need to reply within a specific period of time. Strictly speaking it is not relevant to the question and may be omitted.

Sample Answer F

Again, based on a real answer.

Jade and Small Architects
Fallow Way
Elton,
HP 44 3ND

FOA J Broadbent esq.
TK Construction PLC
Crooks Lane Industrial Estate,
Benton,
Bucks,
HP 42 RU8

Ref.

9th March 2014

Dear Sirs,

GK Pharma, Extension to Sywell Headquarters Building.

We write in connection with TK Construction PLC's (TKC) letter dated 7th March 2014 seeking an extension of time under the JCT Standard Building Contract with Quantities 2011 edition (SB/Q). In the letter TKC request an 8 week extension of time on the following grounds:

1- Exceptionally bad weather conditions over the early winter period.
2- Delays in the release and receipt of the door schedule. TKC claim this information was supplied three weeks later than the date set in the information release schedule.
3- An extended delivery period on the Plasticrete resin flooring specified in the contract documents.

Under the Contract we are obliged to reach a decision on any entitlement to an extension of time that TKC may have on the grounds notified under this letter within 12 weeks of the date of their letter. Our preliminary view and comments on each of these grounds are as follows:

Good references to the contract clauses and a good demonstration of the effect of these clauses.

A clause reference (cl. 2.29.7) would be better.

It is not advisable to end with a question like this. It is simpler to ask for the information.

Good. This closes the issue and also draws attention to the requirement to work in accordance with the programme and contract documents.

Good. This also shows that the student knows the time limitation for considering a request for an extension of time – 12 weeks.

Again, it finishes formally.

1- Exceptionally bad weather conditions

Under clause 2.29.9 of the contract this can be deemed a Relevant Event if the weather conditions are proved to be exceptionally adverse. Very bad weather that you did not foresee when you prepared your programme will not be sufficient. Therefore we request that you provide further details of the 'exceptionally adverse weather conditions' experienced on site and under clause 2.28.2 of the contract provide us with specific 'particulars of its expected effect'. We therefore request that TKC submit a programme indicating when the exceptionally adverse weather conditions occurred in comparison to works on site and the total duration of time attributable to this item. Until this is received we cannot consider this element of your claim.

2- Delays in the release and receipt of the door schedule

Jade & Small Architects acknowledge the claim that the release of the door schedule was three weeks later than noted within the information release schedule. For clarification, please will TKC provide Jade & Small Architects with the date you are claiming this was received by?

3- Plasticrete resin flooring

Our view is that this does not constitute a Relevant Event under clause 2.29. As such there is not entitlement to an extension of time under the Contract. We note it is the contractor's responsibility to complete the works in a timely manner and to manage the works programme in accordance with the contract documents.

Therefore in order that we can reach a decision as to any entitlement that TKC may have to a fair and reasonable extension of time we require further information, clarification and explanation including back up details as noted above at your earliest convenience.

Should we receive no further submissions by the 30th May 2011 then we will proceed to make a decision on the information available.

Yours sincerely,

James Robertson RIBA
Director
For and on Behalf of Jade and Small Architects Ltd

Commentary on Answer F

This is a much better answer and shows the student has good knowledge, knows how to apply it and the professional competence to prepare an appropriate response. The student shows that s/he can work with the scenario and refer to the relevant contract clauses. At no point has the student rushed into a decision or taken sides. S/he also shows an ability to go slightly beyond the problem by reminding the contractor of his wider duties under the contract to carry out the works 'in a timely manner'.

Tips for tackling scenario problems

One technique for rapidly visualising the content issues is to use a 'mind map'. This is a much freer technique than a list-based approach, which can lead to a 'textbook' answer. You can, of course, use this method for any problem-based question.

In this question you need to work with the extension of time clauses in SBC11 and, briefly, the loss and expense clauses. The mind map helps you to get these down in no particular order initially and then make connections between them.

So that you do not underestimate the task, the example given took at least three iterations and used both the contract and one of the key contract guides as points of reference.[5] (In this type of 'open book' examination you can refer to both the contract and the appropriate guide.) Practice this technique by applying it to both sample examination questions and real problems in your workplace.

From the mind map you can now list out the key points which can serve as the basis for the explanatory memo asked for in the question.

1.0 The letter
The contractor's letter is an extension of time notice under cl. 2.27.1 contract administrator.

    1.1   However, 'Has the contractor notified you *'forthwith'*? 'No – certainly not in the case of the weather.' Therefore the notice for this event – and possibly the others – might be invalid. (Note: you do not need to decide this definitively. If you do, you are unlikely to be penalised for getting it wrong – it is the comprehensiveness of the process that the examiner is looking for.)

    1.2 Has the contractor provided sufficient information generally?' 'No.'
Your response should be to say so in your reply – and to ask for more details as set out below.

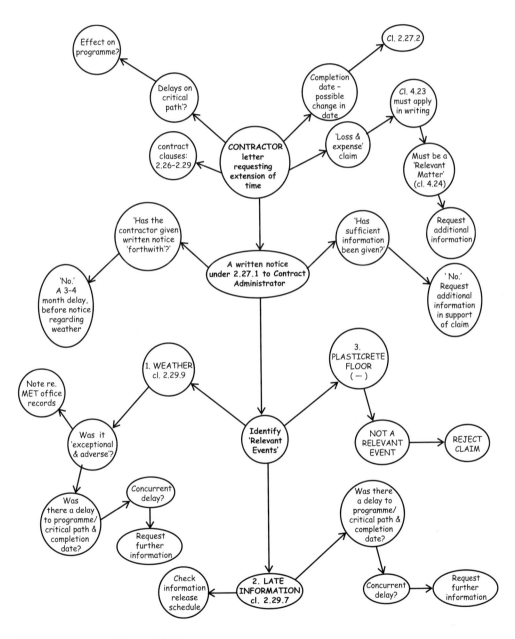

FIGURE 3.2 Extension of time mind map

2.0 The events referred to in the letter

2.1 Bad weather

If the weather is 'exceptional and adverse' then this is a Relevant Event under cl. 2.29.9. If not then it is not valid. Here you must ask for evidence to substantiate the validity of the claim. (Note: you might refer to the Met Office records here for the data and to help *you* decide but in practice you would not do this in the letter but you would in the briefing memo.)

The contractor also needs to state what activity (or activities) was affected by the weather.

2.2 Late information

This is a Relevant Event under cl. 2.29.7. ('Any impediment or default…') and would include failure to provide the schedule by the agreed time stated on the information release schedule. You still need more information regarding the actual delay caused.

2.3 Plasticrete floor

This is not a Relevant Event and the claim can be dismissed. You do not need to add a justification but you may explain in your memo that it is the contractor's duty to manage his domestic subcontractors and suppliers to meet the agreed programme and completion date.

3.0 Effect on Completion Date

3.1 There is an obligation on the contractor to provide evidence to prove that the Relevant Events have changed the agreed Completion Date.

The contractor must relate the delays to the programme and show that specific activities were planned, that they were delayed and that the delay adversely affected the programme.

The delays may be sequential or they may be concurrent.

3.2 Insufficient information

The contractor must provide evidence for each and every part of the claim.

Here he claims a total of eight weeks without explaining how this is arrived at. You need to ask for a reasonable level of detail so that you, as contract administrator, can make a fair and reasonable assessment of the claim.

4.0 Loss and expense

4.1 Claims can only be made for the relevant matters listed in 4.24. These are where the loss and expense are due to the employer. In this case the delay in issuing drawings is relevant (as you are acting as the employer's agent).

The contractor must submit evidence and show that he has taken reasonable steps to mitigate his loss.[6] You might say that the quantum will be decided by the employer's quantity surveyor.

Once these points are compiled, the memo can be drafted relatively quickly with a simple introduction and suggested action points.

You will now see that the rapid analysis using the mind map has resulted in you reassessing the Answer F. It missed a few points, mostly related to the loss and expense part of the claim. On balance, though, it is a very good answer.

EXAMPLE 4, 5 AND 6

The following are some examples of shorter questions and answers that are sometimes included in the written examination.

Question 4

To: Candidate

From: James M

Re: A bit of advice please

Dear Candidate

I am sorry to burden you with this as I know you are busy in the office and I know my absence hasn't helped, but I received a phone call from my cousin late last night, he was in a terrible state and asking my advice. As I understand it the problem goes like this:

Six months ago my cousin retired and he and his wife set off on a long awaited trip around the world. Just before they left new neighbour's moved in next door (they live in a substantial terraced property in Langdon) and popped round to say that they wanted to build an extension across the whole of the rear of their property, much the same as my cousin's extension. My cousin could see no objection and indeed saw the benefit of their extension attaching to their own in terms of reducing heat loss. So much so that he wrote a letter (a copy is attached) for them to send in support of their planning application knowing that he would be away when it was submitted.

In the meantime, his nephew, stayed intermittently at the house, and on one occasion was visited by the neighbour's architect who told him that the work was about to start next door but that there was nothing to worry about as my cousin had given his approval to all the work taking place.

My cousin arrived back last night after what I gather was a very tiring flight from Singapore to find that water had poured into his extension damaging the plasterwork to the adjoining wall, the timber floor and most upsetting of all ruining a painting of some value.

As there was little he could do at that time of night I promised to call back today to advise him of what to do next but his questions were:

1. What procedures should the neighbour and his architect have followed?
2. Who should my cousin claim against?
3. How would he complain about the architect and what might be the likely outcome?

If you could possibly make some notes for me it would be really helpful.

Kind regards

James.

Guidance on answering question 4

The purpose of this question is to test the candidate's knowledge of the Party Wall Act 1996 and to appreciate the architect's responsibility both to their client and third parties and to understand the consequences of not doing so.

That said, personally I would be advising James's cousin to simply contact his insurers and let them liaise with the neighbours and his insurers – I would certainly award points for this pragmatic stance.

However the question does set specific questions.

1. What procedures should the neighbours and his architect have followed
    a. A Party Wall Surveyor should have been appointed. The architect could reasonably be expected to advise the client of this requirement.
    b. A Party Wall Notice should have been issued two months before the planned start date of the work.

c. Given the absence of James's cousin it was likely that the response would not have been received within 14 days and therefore a dispute will have been regarded to have arisen.

NB – The letter to the planning department could not be considered as consent as it refers to agreement 'in principle' as was not in response to a written notice.

d. Despite the architect speaking to the nephew it seems that no attempt was made to contact James's cousin and so at the very least an 'agreed' surveyor (not the architect) should have been appointed.
e. Clearly a Party Wall Award should have been drawn up.

2. Who should the cousin claim against. This is a matter that should be left to the insurers because there is insufficient information to determine this and:
a. The adjoining owner will hold the insurance.
b. The contractor has probably been negligent in the execution of the work.
c. The architects appeals to have been negligent in following due procedures.
d. There may be a fault in the detailing etc.

3. How would he complain about the architects and what might be the likely outcome?

The most appropriate body to complain to would be ARB. A complaint is considered against the code and standards (2010) and whether there is evidence of unacceptable professional conduct or serious professional incompentence. If the ARB concludes that it is likely that there is a case to answer the architect may be prosecuted under the Architects Act 1997. The investigation panel will decide whether to:
a. Dismiss the complaint.
b. Give the architect a cautionary warning.
c. Refer it to the Professional Conduct Committee, the outcome of which could be:
    i.   A reprimand.
    ii. A fine (max £5000).
    iii. Suspension from the register up to 2 years.
    iv. Removal from the register.

Question 5
Interoffice memo

Date: 6th March 2014

To: Candidate

From: Barbra K

Re: Kat Academy

The Governors of Kat Academy have commissioned your practice as architects for their new £2m Science Block project. The Academy Principal told me recently that he has recently recruited a new Premises Manager who is very capable at maintaining the current building stock but unfortunately has little experience in managing and procuring major new-build projects.

However, the Premises Manager will be our primary contact for the Science Block. The Principle has asked whether I can provide some guidance notes for their new Premises Manager to help him understand his role as Client on this project. The notes should help him understand his role during the briefing process, procurement, construction period, and practical completion.

Please can you draft a series of bullet points which can serve as a checklist and which are tailored to this specific project. Try and keep the list to not more than three A4 pages.

Guidance on answering question 5

Issues specific to this school-related client may include the following topics. The Plan of Work provides a useful structure for your answer.

Briefing stage: (Stages 0 and 1)
Cost:
Define the budget – does the £2m include works, professional fees, fitting-out, and even site acquisition?
VAT?
Planning/building regulation fees
What consultants are required and how and when are they to be paid?

Time:
Are there specific dates when school requires the building, e.g. before start of a new term?

What work will school itself have to carry out (equipping, loose furniture) before the room becomes habitable?

Are there specific dates when any noisy works cannot take place (exams)?

Will deliveries have to occur outside of students' arrival/departure times?

Will the process have to relate to dates of Governors' meetings for any specific approvals?

Quality:

CDM obligations

Will the science block have to include space for theory teaching or just laboratory spaces?

Will the block require separate labs for biology, physics and chemistry or mixed use spaces?

Disability and equality provision

Flexibility of space – will it require remodelling periodically?

Any innovative features?

Procurement stage: (Stages 0 and 1)

Calculation of liquidated damages

Insurances

Preferred contractors for tender list

Construction stage: (Stage 5)

Attendance at site meetings

Client not to issue instructions to workers on site

Arrangements for site visits

Personal Protection Equipment

Payment obligations (especially if signatories are absent during summer holiday)

Practical completion: (Stage 6)

Witnessing commissioning and issuing of maintenance manuals

Insurance

Arrangements for reporting defects

In use: (Stage 7)

Post-occupancy administration

Sustainability checkpoints

Question 6

Interoffice memo

Date: 6th March 2014

To: Candidate

From: Practice Director

Re: Designer's Health and Safety Risks and Responsibilities

I have noted recently, the increased number of articles regarding site accidents in the construction press.

Also a colleague told me about an accident on one of their sites which resulted in serious injuries to two demolition contractors.

He said that the whole construction team was interviewed separately by the Health and Safety Executive which he attended with his lawyer.

I'm concerned about what our practice insurance covers.

How do we protect the practice and our staff from the consequences of litigation?

When can we as designers be pursued through the criminal and civil courts? What are the respective circumstances?

Who pays for court/lawyer costs? If the action results in a fine who pays? Is the action against the individual or the practice?

Please draft a report that I can share and discuss with my fellow Directors. I would also expect it to help our professional indemnity insurance renewal discussion.

Guidance on answering question 6

This question is about Health and Safety in the widest sense.

1. A criminal conviction can result in a heavy fine for a company (as well as an individual) can result in a heavy fine or even imprisonment. Prosecution may be followed by actions in the civil courts by those looking for compensation for fatalities or personal injuries or by clients seeking to recover losses (either property related or financial) arising out of the incident on site.

2. Furthermore if the designer is found guilty in a criminal prosecution, they will not inevitably be liable in civil action. However, a criminal conviction is admissible evidence in civil action. If acquitted during a criminal prosecution, it does not follow that they will successfully defend a civil action.

3. The normal rules needed to demonstrate negligence or breach of contract apply to civil actions. So far as designers are concerned, the requisite elements can be summarised as follows:

    > Has there been failure to exercise reasonable skill and care or a breach of a contractual obligation?
    > If so, has someone suffered loss or damage and was this the reasonable foreseeable consequence of the designer's conduct?
    > Was the loss or damage caused by the breach of duty or did it occur for another reason?

4. Criminal prosecutions are different. The standard of care in a civil action is the standard of an ordinary competent person of that profession: that of reasonable average. The standard imposed by health and safety legislation is higher. For example, section 3(2) of the Health and Safety at Work Act 1974 requires employers (including designers) to conduct their undertakings in such a way as to ensure that persons who may be affected are not exposed to risks to their health and safety. In a criminal prosecution the burden will be on the designer to prove that they have taken all reasonably practical measures to ensure health and safety. In a civil claim the burden is on the claimant to prove, on the balance of probabilities, that the designer has been negligent.

5. Practical differences exist between the two different types of legal action. In civil claims, a designer can seek to reduce his or her liability by claiming contributory negligence or negligence by another. Although a designer can seek to blame others for an incident on site, this may be of little effect where health and safety responsibilities are placed on all those involved in construction projects. A designer can attempt to settle a civil claim, for example by negotiating, formal offers of settlement or mediation. Criminal prosecutions are destined for trial.

6. A designer can insure against all the damages and costs incurred in a civil action whereas in a criminal prosecution there is no insurance against fines or prosecution costs but a designer may be able to insure against his defence costs. Within professional indemnity insurance cover liability can be excluded or limited in a contract, but such terms will be of little use in a criminal prosecution.

EXAMPLES 7 AND 8

These are some examples of short, essentially knowledge-based questions and answers which give a good indication of the level of detail for a good answer. They are testing wider areas of knowledge and understanding in the Professional Criteria.

Question 7

'Explain what is meant by the term 'Privity of Contract' and give an example to illustrate how it applies'.

A model answer might be as follows:

The doctrine of privity of contract states that only the parties to a contract are bound by its terms. Under the doctrine any person who is not a party to the contract cannot confer rights or impose obligations in the contract. Also, only parties to the contract can sue or be sued for a breach of contract – so parties outside the contract but who may suffer from a failure of the parties to perform their duties under the contract – cannot make a claim for damages under the terms of the contract.

For example, if you buy an apartment in a new block you have no contractual link with the architect or the contractor or any of the subcontractors. The only contract is with the developer who commissioned the block. If there is a failure then – under the doctrine of privity of contract – you can only make a contractual claim against the developer. He would then have to make a claim against the contractor and/or the architect.

However, the Contracts (Rights of Third Parties) Act 1999 allows named third parties in the contract to enforce the terms of the contract. The Act has to be included in the contract terms and is not a universal right. Many contracts exclude the Act, for example, the RIBA Standard Conditions of Appointment {clause 7.8}.

A collateral warranty will create a separate contract between the contractor, for example, and the purchaser and therefore give the new purchaser the right to make a claim under that contract.

(Separate collateral warranties would be required with the architect and engineers for the design.)

SBC11 gives two options that give third parties rights to make a claim either under the 1999 Act or the use of a separately published collateral warranty.

The answer demonstrates an adequate knowledge for the purposes of meeting the Part 3 Criteria of the principle of 'privity of contract' – based on lecture notes and further reading of standard reference texts. This in itself would not be enough for a good answer but the example shows how the principles can be applied and this shows the candidate's understanding of the subject in a practical sense. The references to the Contracts (Rights of Third Parties) Act 1999 shows further knowledge and understanding of how statutes can affect contracts. This Act is unusual in that it has to be agreed to be adopted as a contract condition – it is not an implied term that applies regardless.

The reference to the RIBA Standard Conditions of Appointment shows a deeper knowledge of how the Act can apply.

Collateral warranties are relevant as they provide a separate contract. The level of detail here is about right for this question – but is an important subject in itself.

Lastly the reference to the options in SBC11 show how both the 1999 Act and collateral warranties are used in standard building contracts.

Question 8
What is professional indemnity insurance and why is it important?

A model answer would be as follows:

Professional indemnity insurance is a type of third party liability insurance. It does not give any benefits to the architect directly but you are covered by the policy for claims against you. The extent of the cover depends on the wording of the policy. A typical policy will cover you up to an agreed limit for any sum that you are legally liable to pay made during the period of the insurance. This includes payments due as a result of a breach of contract with a client – or a claim for negligence.

The cover is normally limited to the architect's 'reasonable skill and care' in carrying out his or her professional duties. Therefore 'fitness for purpose' obligations are specifically excluded – as are liquidated damages.

It is important that professional indemnity insurance is renewed annually as claims are made in the year of the claim – not the year the problem occurred. It is also important that retired architects have 'run off' insurance cover in place to cover claims that may occur during the liability period – typically 6 or 12 years.

The insurance is important as it provides a benefit to clients and users. This importance is recognised by both the RIBA and the ARB.

The RIBA refer to the need for professional indemnity insurance in its Code of Conduct Guidance Note 5 and it is referred to in RIBA Standard Agreements. Standard 8 of the ARB Code and Standards (2010) states that architects are expected to have adequate professional indemnity insurance cover.

'The Board recommends that the minimum limit of indemnity provided by professional indemnity insurance should be £250,000 for each and every claim. It is important to note that architects should maintain sufficient cover to enable them to meet claims arising from professional practice and bear in mind that claims may arise from personal injury as well as loss, damage, delay and additional costs.' (ARB PII Guidance: www.arb.org.uk/pii-guidance)

Failure to maintain adequate cover is a disciplinary matter and may lead to action by the RIBA or prosecution under the Architects Act 1997 for Unacceptable Professional Conduct or Serious Professional Incompetence.

Insurance law is highly complex. Therefore it is important that you show you understand the basics. You are not expected to know more than the professional requirements although in practice clients will require greater cover to be taken out unless you are a sole practitioner. To that effect the RIBA can provide cover that meets the ARB requirements.

This answer covers the important points relating to professional indemnity insurance. You would not normally be expected to quote from sources in such detail – the ARB requirements have been included for completeness.

(Note: with reference to the 'CIC Liability Briefing' (2008) at www.cic.ork.uk/liability)

Conclusions

You should now be aware of the different types of written examination paper and different question formats. This chapter has given you some pointers as to what makes a good answer and the level of detail with which you need to be familiar. The discussion of the different types of question and how to approach them should assist you in preparing for the written examinations. Hopefully it will be clear that examiners are looking for the application of knowledge by a competent, practising professional rather than knowledge taken out of context. Therefore the process you follow is as important as the knowledge you can demonstrate. You should also be able to distinguish between what is relevant and what is not, another valuable professional skill.

How your written examination answers are used in the oral examination is explored in Chapter 5.

Finally, you should be aware that thorough preparation and time management both before and during the written examinations are key factors in your success.

THE CASE STUDY
CHAPTER 4

This chapter covers the role of the case study in the RIBA Part 3 examination. It includes:

> how to select a suitable project;
> how to plan its structure and its content;
> the place of critical analysis in the study; and
> some pointers towards success based on professional examiner feedback.

The case study is essentially work-based. Part 3 course leaders are very aware of the importance of gaining the right experience on the appropriate project and will be able to advise students on project selection and personal involvement. You may receive guidance and support from your school of architecture, but you will not produce a satisfactory case study without the involvement and support of your practice.

A very small minority of schools of architecture do not require a case study to be prepared for the Part 3 examination. In these cases the requirements of the examination are met in other ways; principally by a range of assignments and/or detailed documents extensively analysing a fictitious scenario. This chapter will help you to understand the value of the case study as both a learning device and an assessment tool.

The case study can seem daunting, partly because of the amount of work involved but also because this is the element in which practice and theory come together. What your practice can offer in terms of a subject for the study and what the Part 3 examiners require from the study are sometimes frighteningly mismatched. Inevitably, the commercial needs of your practice rarely dovetail with your needs as a student and this has the potential to cause friction. Each student therefore needs to work closely with his or her practice to gain the cooperation of the office, ready access to the source material, relevant project experience and the scope to utilise the opportunities in an effective way.

The role of the case study in the Part 3 examination

The case study is the vehicle for demonstrating your knowledge and understanding of the professional, regulatory, procurement, contractual and management issues covered by the Professional Criteria. In addition, you must also demonstrate your professional judgement through your critical analysis of and reflection on the events and incidents that the study incorporates. In order to meet the requirements of the Professional Criteria your case study should also include post-mobilisation events and contract administration, and it should therefore follow a project's life cycle as comprehensively as possible from inception to completion. The RIBA Plan of Work maps out the key Work Stages and you should aim to experience and cover each Work Stage in your case study in order to fulfil the key elements of the Criteria. (Note: some Part 3 providers assess post-mobilisation events and contract administration thoroughly in specific coursework assignments or office-based written examinations. This gives greater freedom with project selection. Check with your course leader/PSA before selecting the project you are going to study.)

Getting started

The issues to take into account when selecting your case study can be summarised by the following points:

> the economic environment and the challenges facing the office as a business enterprise;
> the type and scale of projects;
> the 'maturity' of the office and the office culture;
> office specialisms and 'niches';
> the type of clients;
> the range of conventional services provided;
> relationships with clients;
> types of agreement between client and architect;
> time taken for projects to move from outline enquiry to mobilisation;
> the chosen procurement route;
> the type of construction contract;
> the post-mobilisation project timescale.

Your competence, as well as your experience, will influence the willingness and ability of the office to support you through the process. Assessing your own value, experience, expertise, responsibilities and involvement in projects is an important part of choosing the right case study.

A good starting point is to apply the same rules to the case study as you would to any other written project, establishing a beginning, middle and end. You can prepare by carrying out a short feasibility study of two or three possible projects, examining the available options and suitability, and considering your own potential involvement. The framework that follows details how, for this initial study, you would consider the above general factors within the context of the Part 3 case study.

CASE STUDY FEASIBILITY PROPOSAL

Project details

> Practice: name and background
> Project selection: type and value
> The client
> The appointment
> Project timetable and programme
> Student's role and responsibilities
> The office design team
> The project team (consultants, etc.)
> Town planning and regulatory issues
> Procurement and contract choice
> Mobilisation
> Works on site
> Issues, challenges, details
> Areas of interest: disputes
> Problems in project execution

Personal programme

> An estimation of feasibility and programme:
    − Is it achievable?
    − Does the project programme link favourably to the Part 3 programme?
> Assessment of complexity and scale:
    − Is it too large or complex?
    − Can the study be reduced in scope to one or two parts of the total project?
> Negotiation:
    − Can the office allocate me to the project, and if so in what capacity?
> Agreement with the office on the aims of the study:
    − Do I have enough support from the office?
> Time-management issues:
    − Will my other commitments allow sufficient time to carry out the work?
    − What are the key dates in the programme?

> Data collection:
>   - How accessible, accurate, clear and complete will the data be?
>   - Do I need cooperation from individuals outside the office; for example, from members of the project team?
> Structure and format:
>   - Have I allowed enough time for presentation and checking?
> Issues to raise at tutorials and in the office.
> Monitoring personal progress and development.
> Further reading and research.

Clearly, two factors are critical to the success of the case study:

1. Negotiating your involvement in a suitable project with the office; and
2. Managing personal time effectively during the case study.

Frequently raised issues

The case study can be categorised as *work-based learning*. The interplay between the professional and commercial demands of the office, the requirements of Part 3, and your personal competence, responsibilities and motivation will inevitably create some friction regardless of the commitment of the office to supporting your professional development. Both parties need to be aware of this potential tension. Part 3 course leaders and their teaching teams see this as part of the territory. They can offer advice but will rarely be actively involved in what is essentially an element of the implied contract between employer and employee. The complex nature of the case study situation gives rise to a number of issues that can impact on the success of the study. Try to get a summary to your course leader as soon as possible so that s/he can comment on your proposal.

AN INCOMPLETE PROJECT LIFE CYCLE

The RIBA Plan of Work has many uses in the case study. It provides a good starting point for checking the completeness of a study's planned content and structure. In order to meet the Professional Criteria the study must cover some post-mobilisation issues and contract administration in particular. The study must also include what can be termed 'the dynamics of the contract'. This includes valuation, interim certification and, if possible, practical completion as well as the routine and non-routine events that occur during any construction contract: unforeseen events, variations and instructions, and delays leading to a variety of claims. A study that does not include the post-mobilisation phase is very unlikely to succeed as it will omit one of the key topics of the Professional Criteria: PC5 Building Procurement unless this is assessed comprehensively elsewhere at Part 3 – by written assignment, for example.

This leads to a number of options:

1. Delaying completion of the study in order to ensure that these essential areas are covered.
2. Switching to a different project for the post-mobilisation phase.
3. Shadowing a suitable project.

The simplest course is to delay the study but this should be agreed in conjunction with the office and the school of architecture. These potential problems emphasise the need to anticipate and address these issues at the feasibility stage. It is very difficult for you to catch up later and try to compensate for unforeseen events.

A TALE OF TWO PROJECTS

Considering two projects in your case study is a legitimate approach. However, it is significantly more difficult. You need to be very clear at which point you are changing the subject of the study. The principal problem is that you have to absorb and analyse two sets of events which are likely to be independent and lack any common themes. The danger is that gaps will occur and necessary areas will simply not be covered. Examiners also have to be satisfied that you understand both the scenarios. The best approach is to ensure that the areas of the studies which you are considering match the Work Stages of the Plan of Work. You should also be prepared for duplication of effort on your part and concern within the office that your efforts are being spread too thinly. This also assumes active involvement in both projects, which adds to the complexity of the challenge. The alternative is to shadow the post-mobilisation (or pre-mobilisation) phases.

THE DIVERSITY OF CONSTRUCTION CONTRACTS

The term 'contracts' is applied not only to building contracts but also to professional services contracts. A common criticism of Part 3 is that the Professional Criteria are skewed towards the concept of the sole practitioner in a traditional role as client adviser, designer, lead consultant, project manager and contract administrator – and therefore fail to give sufficient recognition to the full range of architectural practice and the wider changes in the construction industry. These criticisms include the range and scope of professional agreements (or contracts) for architectural services, the different methods of procurement and the wide range of building contracts used in the public and private sectors and for international projects.[1]

As a result, some students and architectural practices question the need to teach and assess more traditional client agreements and construction contracts where the architect retains the role of lead consultant. This attitude tends to miss four key points:

1. Many small and medium-sized architectural practices, their clients and building contractors use standard agreements for professional services and JCT agreements for construction projects. These contractual arrangements are satisfactory and appropriate where it is assumed that the architect will act as lead consultant.
2. The profession in general and senior decision-makers in particular will use industry-standard agreements as the benchmark from which to carry out their own comparative analyses of the new roles, responsibilities and liabilities that arise out of the new range of agreements that are currently being used.
3. Most practices, including the main international 'signature' practices, started as small enterprises and a small but significant number of newly registered architects will set up in practice as sole practitioners. The profession recognises the aspirations of these individuals but it also requires that the public can expect competent service from even the newest architects on the register.[2]
4. Legal concepts and contract law are universal and so are the skills required to apply them to construction contracts, regardless of whether the agreements are 'traditional' or not.

The complex nature of current architectural practice dictates that you will experience a variety of contracts. With over 40 per cent of construction contracts being let using some form of design and build agreement, a significant minority of students will be working in this type of project environment. Beyond a certain contract value and complexity it is very unlikely that the architect will remain as lead consultant in the conventional sense.[3]

You should be aware of the following issues both at the planning stage of your study and during your case study's development and discuss them on a regular basis with your office, mentor and tutor.

Complexity

The complexity of project organisation and scale, together with the likely effect on project timescales, needs to be considered carefully. At a basic level, understanding the complexity of a project can be time-consuming. Condensing this into a case study may be impractical. For example, past students have written good studies of PFI/PF2 projects but have failed to meet the requirements of Part 3 because their studies were incomplete. Too much time and effort was spent 'telling the story'. In these complex project environments it is sometimes difficult to fully understand the nature and extent of the architect's involvement and the terms of their agreement with the client or clients. Different layers are introduced into the client organisation: project managers, employer representatives, contract administrators.

A successful strategy for dealing with contractual complexities is to select different parts of the project for detailed analysis and to set those parts within the context of the whole project.

Involvement

Design and build contracts, complex management contracts and projects for major housebuilders and urban regeneration clients all require different levels of involvement from the design team. In particular, the all-important post-mobilisation phases of the project tend to be the province of the contracting organisation and the architect's input may be limited or non-existent.

A successful strategy will employ comparative analysis. All construction contracts, regardless of their complexity and drafting, share what can be termed the same 'dynamics'. Whether the architect is involved or not, certain processes take place. Variations and unforeseen events occur. Costs of variations need to be agreed. Health and safety matters must be addressed. Works end and, hopefully, the final account is agreed. Except in the smallest project, these processes may be either fragmented or opaque to you, as a member of the design team, unless you are tasked with specific aspects of the project. Your site involvement may be limited, if required at all. It is normally possible to discuss these processes with one of the contract's project managers. Thorough preparation before any meeting is vital to your understanding of the post-mobilisation aspects of the project. A comparative analysis can then be made, discussing the actual project processes in terms of standard JCT procedures as well as comparing the roles of the independent contract administrator in the JCT forms and, for example, the project surveyor employed directly by the client-contractor.

Scope of the architect's appointment

The role of the architect varies between appointments. It is important that you are aware of the main characteristics of the relationship between architect and client. The architect's contract and the construction contract are inevitably very closely linked. This is not always apparent and, because they tend to be taught separately, you may fail to be aware of or understand the link. The RIBA's Standard Form of Agreement (the contract between the architect and the client), is itself a menu with various alternatives. Bespoke agreements will limit the scope of the architectural services to, for example, detailed design only. The scope of services will be reflected in the agreed fee. You should be able to compare what was agreed with a model agreement such as the RIBA form.[4]

SHADOWING

The term 'shadowing' means that you are not working on the project that is the subject of your case study but are obtaining and evaluating project experience 'second hand'. In terms of meeting the Criteria, this is an acceptable approach to the case study but it is a compromise and should really only be considered as a last resort. At a practical, office level the main contention is that, as an employee and fee earner, you cannot be working effectively on the project to which you have been employed to contribute and shadowing another project at the same time. If you are able to fully experience the project that you are shadowing by attending design and construction team meetings and visiting the construction site, then you will not be available for similar meetings on your main project. Carrying out the 'desktop' research required, trawling through files to obtain background information on the client, the appointment and the statutory consents, even if carried out outside normal working hours, will be time-consuming. There is also an element of simple distraction from your main employment, as well as conflicts and diary clashes between projects. Inevitably, your main project will take precedence.

The question of remoteness may pose additional problems in that the further you get from actual 'live' project experience in both time and space, the more difficult it becomes to:

> obtain and collate the necessary data; and
> analyse and evaluate the recorded events.

The resultant case study may become a dry record or diary of events, the completeness of their retelling being dependent on the completeness of the office records. Alternatively, it might read as a building study seen in the pages of one of the professional journals with a description of the product rather than an analysis of the process. Also, returning to the concept of the case study as a vehicle for analysis, the more distant the events in time, the more likely it is that the legislative and contract environments, rules and procedures will have changed. Finally, from the author's experience as a teacher and examiner, it is more difficult and requires more effort and time to achieve a similar result by shadowing a project than it is by actively working on one.

INTERNATIONAL PROJECTS

A significant number of architectural offices of varying sizes are international in ownership and/or outlook. Historically, a small number of well-known UK offices have derived a significant proportion of their workload from overseas projects. The growth of international practices using the UK as a springboard into the rest of the EU has also increased the number of overseas projects.

The trend towards globalisation generally and the breaking down of restrictive trade barriers has supported the increase in international projects. The challenge for you in using an international project as the subject of your case study is that Part 3 is a UK qualification and the case study has to address UK issues. It follows that assessment will be on knowledge and understanding of UK regulations, practice and management issues, procurement and contract administration. You may also face the same type of problems concerning remoteness from the contractual action and the 'dynamics' of the contract discussed above in the section on shadowing.

International projects are likely to be large and complex, employing different contract procedures and partial architectural services. UK architects are likely to be working with local architects who will deal with detailed local issues such as regulatory constraints and contract administration.

Despite these problems, international projects can produce excellent case studies, provided it is clearly understood that success lies in the use of comparative analysis. This involves assessing the local experience, regulations and contractual arrangements and then comparing them with 'normal' UK practice. The comparative method will be discussed in more detail below as it provides an essential key to constructive analysis of any project and is a powerful means of demonstrating knowledge and understanding of 'best practice' in architecture and construction. (The use of 'best practice' models or examples is important because they show the level of knowledge and competence that a registered architect would be expected to follow in order to meet the professional standards set out by the ARB and RIBA Codes.) One student recently successfully analysed a project based in Rotterdam with a UK 'signature' design architect, a local Dutch architectural practice, a Dutch professional services agreement subdividing the work, a Dutch planning process and a management contract.

Another took as its subject a large international airport in Damascus with a UK design architect, international subcontractors and management contractor. Insurance required American construction and fire regulations. Health and safety regulations were not as rigorous as the CDM Regulations and, as perhaps to be expected in Syria, the planning process bore little resemblance to the democratic processes followed in the UK.

Dominatrix punished for poor fire safety

A DOMINATRIX who runs a dungeon in which men are chained up, gagged and whipped, has been fined £5,000 for breaching fire safety laws.

Lorraine White, 41, was prosecuted by the fire service after crews struggled to gain entry to her "Medusa club" following a blaze in a leaking gas heater.

Crews who were called to the basement on an industrial estate in Stockport, Greater Manchester, found handcuffs, chains and other restraining devices, the town's magistrates heard.

There was only one manually operated fire alarm and one fire exit that was permanently locked. Fire investigators also found several canisters of nitrous oxide, or laughing gas, which was inhaled by White's clients, the court heard.

When questioned, White said she had no idea that she was responsible for fire safety arrangements.

Elizabeth Dudley-Jones, prosecuting, said: "She was asked what would happen if there was a fire when her clients were under the influence of the gas and restrained. She said she had not considered it."

White said she earned about £1,100 a month from men paying for "slight bondage" at the club. "It involved a lot of humiliation, doing domestic work and dressing up in women's clothes," added Ms Dudley-Jones.

White, a former beautician from Salford, pleaded guilty to four charges of breaching fire safety rules. She was fined £5,000 and ordered to pay £3,000 costs and a £120 victim charge.

Peter Grogan, defending, said White had spent £10,000 refurbishing her dungeon and it now fully complied with fire safety requirements.

Peter O'Reilly, a fire prevention officer, said: "No matter what business you may have, you must take fire safety seriously."

Daily Telegraph
14th April 2014[5]

In comparing architectural practice with Lorraine White's rather older profession, it is interesting to remember that Lorraine, a 'Madame', considered that the practices that routinely took place in her 'lock-up' on an industrial estate in Stockport were neither out of the ordinary nor illegal. Without going into too much detail, tying up senior members of society who should have known better (with their consent) and then charging them for the privilege (plus a range of other, more interesting services) was an everyday occurrence and relatively humdrum. Lorraine clearly worked hard to meet her clients' expectations but finally fell foul of the fire regulations and by concentrating on her main work failed to put basic measures in place. Unfortunately in these circumstances, as with Part 3, ignorance of the law and best practice is no excuse. Architectural offices that also develop their own methods consider that their, possibly unprofessional, unethical and sometimes illegal, practices are also the norm.

You will tend to encounter these office practices accidentally. Gradually, it will dawn on you that a particular range of office practices is indeed peculiar and possibly unsuitable for a Part 3 case study. These 'peculiarities' fall into a range of categories, and sometimes you may suffer directly as a result. The main categories concern:

> the practice itself;
> its management;
> regulatory concerns; and
> contract administration.

The first category, practice, often involves 'passing off'. This is where the term 'architect' (a protected title) is used very freely. It is not unusual for a Part 3 student to be described as the 'Project Architect' in correspondence. Sometimes this designation slips into the CV or career appraisal, with predictable results at interview. Such usage may contravene the Architects Act 1997 and be subject to prosecution, but is relatively harmless. More suspect is the senior practitioner who describes himself or herself as an architect when they have never been eligible to be registered in the UK. This is a more serious offence and is likely to indicate other problems with the practice. Fortunately, it is a very infrequent occurrence.

The second category, management, tends to be indicated by two factors:

> lack of paperwork generally; and
> under-resourcing.

This might start with your own contract of employment, or more precisely the lack of it. It may also include routinely failing to confirm appointments for professional services in an appropriate written form. Under-resourcing may be indicated by an inability to meet agreed deadlines and a general lack of organisation. Both practices contravene the ARB Standards.

The third category of irregular practice may include instructing work that has not been granted Planning Consent or Building Regulations approval or failing to apply for the appropriate consent. In the case of Listed Buildings, this is a criminal offence and may also lead to prosecution under the Architects Act 1997 by the ARB.

The fourth category, contract administration, can cover an enormous territory. One problem is confusing 'negotiation' of a building contract with bona fide tendering. Another is the slavish use of one form of JCT agreement (typically Minor Works or the Intermediate Form) without considering its applicability to a particular project. Typical justifications for such action range from the claim, 'We always use this form' to passing the buck for the decision-making to other individuals – often the much-maligned quantity surveyor. Other indicators include poor or non-existent contract administration, acting *ultra vires*,[6] and a reluctance to administer the terms of the contract.

These incidents may be isolated but recur throughout the project life cycle and indicate a poor level of understanding of professional roles and responsibilities. Where these practices are habitual, no one considers that anything is amiss. This presents a range of problems. You will often be one of the least experienced members of the office and it will be difficult initially to recognise and still more difficult to express your concern over these professional and contractual shortcomings. If you are unaware of any shortcomings or readily assume that because certain practices work in that particular office they are generally acceptable, then you will face problems in your analysis of events in the case study.

Having recognised that there may be some unprofessional conduct, how do you discuss it? The general reaction is to drop the project immediately, fearing that the shortcomings of the office will be confused with your own. That confusion will not arise in the minds of examiners provided that the student is aware of the problems and comments on them. It is, therefore, reasonable to document instances of irregular practice if they are relevant to the project. Incidentally, all the examples noted above have been drawn from recent case studies, proving that it does happen.

The tool for effectively handling these, often difficult, incidents is comparative analysis; beginning by recording the event or experience, comparing it with 'best practice' guidelines or models, reaching a conclusion about the experience and making recommendations for the future. This method allows you to identify poor practice and distance yourself from it.

Confidentiality

Architectural projects tend to be the result of private agreements between individuals or organisations who do not expect that their work will be recorded and analysed as part of a professional examination. Confidentiality is an issue, to some degree, in all case studies. Normally it is only a minor consideration but in some studies the sensitive nature of the project, the client or the budget may restrict your ability to disclose key events and even threaten the viability of the study.

Universities and other institutions cannot guarantee confidentiality. At a regulatory level a university may own the students' work and retain it without any restriction on the terms of its use. In practical terms, however, the study also passes through a number of hands. Inevitably, students want to know what makes a good study and will want to read the most successful examples, so tutors may use them as part of their teaching material. University examiners and professional examiners will assess them, external examiners will sample them for quality assurance and standardisation purposes and the professional bodies, the RIBA and the ARB, may sample them for validation and prescription purposes, respectively.

Each project should be considered on its merits. In extreme circumstances names can be changed. Sensitive data such as fee agreements or project budgets might be omitted. In most instances examiners are not interested in the actual hard data or figures but some information is, of necessity, required to allow them to assess your understanding of the main professional issues. Generally you can expect that examiners reading case studies will treat the content with respect and as confidential.

Negotiation, ownership and time management

NEGOTIATION

The importance of discussion and negotiation with your practice with the objective of receiving its full support has already been stated. A thoroughly prepared feasibility proposal will be a persuasive document and diligent background work to flag up the key problems and offer some solutions will allow conversations to be more focused and make the most of the limited time available.

OWNERSHIP

It is important to try to obtain some common ownership of the study by you and your office. This is for a number of reasons. Offices will often agree to support a case study in principle and then fail to give adequate support in practice. This can range from failing to honour access to files or construction sites, not giving adequate time for shadowing, to moving students onto other jobs mid-project to suit the office workload. While you must appreciate the sound, business-led reasons, you should try to communicate the difficulties of juggling the requirements of completing Part 3 and meeting the immediate needs of the practice. Effective communication can ease the tension caused by the sometimes conflicting needs of your professional development and the workload of the practice and lead to a greater likelihood that the office will understand your problems and share the ownership of the study.

TIME MANAGEMENT

Management skills, planning and prioritising are as crucial to the successful completion of Part 3 as professional and legal knowledge. Architectural practices operate to project timetables that are often pre-set and non-negotiable. Part 3 operates in a similar environment but may prove more flexible. Key Part 3 dates, including examinations and hand-in dates, are generally set well in advance. Most universities run to an annual cycle whereas office planning is usually more short term. It is therefore important that you circulate these key dates to relevant people in the office as well as recording them in a personal programme.

University coursework submission rules are generally rigid so you need to work to these key deadlines and try to avoid any clashes. The general reaction from examiners regarding late submission is that it is unprofessional.

Case study structure

Before you can give a comprehensive analysis of a construction project you need to have a clear idea of its structure. As the study develops you should refer back to the outline structure and ensure that all areas are covered and given equal attention and weight. One of the major reasons why case studies fail to meet the requirements of the examiners is incompleteness or serious 'gaps' in the study. It would be unwise, and perhaps impossible, to try to provide a checklist for a standard case study given the wide variety of procurement methods and events that occur in construction projects. However, the following structure should prove useful.

> Project summary
> Introduction
  − an outline of the project
> The project environment
  − the office
  − the client and other stakeholders
  − procurement strategy
  − the appointment
  − the project team
  − design development
  − practice management
  − *critical analysis: Work Stages 0, 1 & 2 (and appointment, etc.)*

> The legislative framework
>   − planning and development
>   − heritage
>   − sustainability
>   − building regulations
>   − health and safety
>   − inclusive design
>   − adjoining owner rights
>   − *critical analysis: Work Stages 3–4*
> Procurement, contract choice and tendering
>   − procurement processes
>   − form of contract
>   − subcontractors and package contractors
>   − tendering procedures
>   − mobilisation
>   − *critical analysis*
> Post-mobilisation
>   − the role of the architect
>   − contract administration
>   − contract events
>   − completion
>   − post-completion
>   − *critical analysis: Work Stages 5–6*
> Conclusions and recommendations for future practice
> References and bibliography

It should be stressed that not all studies need to follow this exact structure or content but if a key area is missing completely then the 'gaps' may be too great to allow the study to pass. You can see that the post-mobilisation phase takes up one-quarter of the study. However, it is unlikely that you will cover all contract administration issues. The form of contract, for example, especially design and build, will make this more difficult and some contractual events, such as practical completion, may not fit into the project timescale.

Length of study

Guidance on the length of the study differs between the various schools of architecture and examination centres. Case study assessors and professional examiners are unanimous in requesting that case studies are comprehensive but as short as possible. Indeed, examiners consider that an excessively long study fails to demonstrate the necessary professional presentation skills and the ability to edit work to make it accessible. You should also remember that professional examiners will typically examine six students in a day and may be required to read and assess six case studies as well as developing a series of relevant questions to ask at the interview. Striking the right balance is therefore important. A suggested target length might be 10,000 words, made up as follows:

> Introduction and project summary: 1000 words;
> The project environment: architect's office, etc: 2000 words;
> Regulatory issues: 2000 words;
> Procurement and contract: 2000 words;
> Post-mobilisation: 2000 words;
> Conclusions and recommendations: 1000 words.

When the study is seen in these terms, with each section probably shorter than most academic assignments at degree level, it appears less daunting and more manageable. It should be stressed that these targets are only guidelines. Recent experience suggests that students write between 8000 and 12,000 words. It is essential that you check with your Part 3 provider. For example RIBA North West and Cardiff University suggest a minimum of 5000 words and not more than 7000 words.

Looking at each section in detail

PROJECT SUMMARY

The project summary should set the scene and allow examiners to pick up on the key characteristics of the project *immediately*. The summary should be limited to one page:

> an illustration of the project
> project title
> location
> client
> project team
> procurement route
> contract type
> value
> start and completion dates.

INTRODUCTION

The introduction should summarise the main issues and explain your role in the project. If the examiners cannot understand your role and involvement they may begin to doubt your understanding of the project. Examiners are all registered architects and think visually so appropriate illustrations will help to convey the nature of the project.

THE OFFICE, THE CLIENT, THE APPOINTMENT, THE PROJECT TEAM, DESIGN DEVELOPMENT AND PRACTICE MANAGEMENT

The office

This section should include some background on the architect's office (or other co-professions' office) and the type of organisation or practice: for example, partnership, limited liability company, limited liability partnership, its size and maturity and the predominant types of work.

The client and other stakeholders

Many projects evolve in a complex environment involving many different stakeholders. Others may have relatively simple decision-making structures, such as a new-build house for an owner-occupier. Some background information on the client is important. For example, many commercial clients operate in very different ways to end-users. Where the structure is complex – typically with public sector projects – it may help to draw a 'stakeholder map' or diagram that shows lines of influence. It may also be relevant to mention other stakeholders, such as end-users, funders and possibly government departments or quangos (see Chapter 1) that have an influence over the project.

Procurement strategy

The procurement strategy may not exist, as such. For example, with residential projects for owner-occupiers a traditional route normally prevails where the architect is lead consultant and contract administrator. In a complex environment the procurement strategy is likely to have been decided very early on – at Latham's 'pre-project' stage[7] – before the architect or the design team has been appointed. In this complexity it is sometimes difficult to determine the exact role of the architect.

Discussing the complex project environment is a challenge – and a balancing exercise. Do you try to give a comprehensive account of the project environment or do you risk giving an incomplete picture by over-simplifying it? It is impossible to generalise as new variations in procurement strategy are constantly evolving. An effective way of explaining this is to provide a diagram showing contractual links and reporting lines supported by a short summary that concentrates on the architect's role.

The explanation of the project environment and procurement choice is important as it will affect the scope of the architect's role and responsibilities, and ultimately the appointment. The following gives a summary of factors that may affect the procurement strategy and may assist you to discuss how the strategy was decided:

> the type of client and their level of sophistication in project management;
> funding requirements;
> the number of parties involved;
> legal, managerial and technical advice;
> the client's attitude to project risk;
> the relevant experience of the project design team;
> project size and budget;
> complexity and possibly the 'one-off' nature of a project;
> timescales (lead-in time to mobilisation, in particular);
> project location (possibly outside the UK);
> procurement processes;
> form of contract;
> subcontractors and package contractors;
> tendering procedures;
> mobilisation.

The appointment

You may not be able to access the details of the appointment but you should be able to establish the type of appointment (standard form or 'bespoke'), for full or partial services and, more importantly, whether or not it is in writing. This is likely to be your first opportunity to discuss your office's practices in the light of 'best practice', model forms of appointment and the profession's Codes and Standards and to apply some comparative analysis to demonstrate your awareness of key relevant professional issues. You should also be able to discuss the agreed fees and payment terms.

In the more complex procurement environment discussed above the terms of the appointment are likely to be more complex too. For the purposes of Part 3 you should be able to explain the scope of your office's services *at that point in the project* in relation to the procurement route together with any other features such as quality control or co-ordination of information. It is also important to note that the procurement route may change and your services may change as a result. In this case you need to be aware of this and comment briefly. It may, for example, change the scope of your professional services. This is particularly true when a management contracting route is considered and it is then changed to design and build – or vice versa. Remember, you are not expected to be an expert but you should be able to express a view. It is important that you are clear about the terminology used. New procurement routes breed new terms. You may need to explain the actual role taken by the architect.

You should also be aware of any other contractual liabilities created by collateral warranties and any sub-consultancy contracts.

Design development

It is very useful to briefly discuss the early RIBA Work Stages and design development in particular as this will create an opportunity to discuss how stakeholders or other factors such as regulations affect the design development. This process may be highly structured or informal. A formal brief may be developed with a high level of fixity or this phase of the project may be more fluid. Each approach affects how the project design develops. It is also the place to discuss how late changes in the brief may affect the design and how different procurement methods change the design development process by, for example, affecting the flow of information to the design team.

Practice management

As you write the case study it will be natural to concentrate on the different RIBA Work Stages. However the Part 3 Criteria cover all aspects of practice management as well as project management. The two processes overlap explicitly at critical points in a project – the appointment, for example, but good management permeates all aspects of a successful and profitable design project; in particular, the planning and management of staff resources. This is, therefore, a good point in the study to discuss how the office resourced the project team and how it managed the client, the other stakeholders and the design team as well as changes in the brief. Experience shows that tension and mismanagement at this stage often has a number of knock-on effects later in the project, such as incomplete production information or resourcing problems.

The project team

The complexity of the team is normally a function of the size of the project and the sophistication of the client. Project team structures may change as the project develops, with some team members being replaced or falling away. It is important to show these changes, especially in design and build contracts where the architect is working for the client or the contractor, or where novation[8] occurs. Simple diagrams are a useful way of showing these relationships.

The Part 3 Criteria also require you to consider how other consultants are appointed. It is unlikely that students will have access to other consultants' fee agreements, but for the purposes of the study you should be able to discuss the contractual relationships between the client and the consultants or any sub-consultancy arrangements that may affect the architect's responsibilities and liabilities.

LEGISLATIVE FRAMEWORK

It is essential to show that you understand the regulatory environment in which professional architects operate. Typically, these issues fall into the following areas:

> planning and development
> heritage
> sustainability
> building regulations
> health and safety
> inclusion
> adjoining owner rights

This list is generic and should be adapted to suit the location and type of project. Remember that this section of the case study shows your knowledge and systematic understanding of the UK legislative framework and its context. Your office and your clients will, in future, rely on your ability to navigate through the relevant legislation and procedures effectively. Therefore with projects located overseas the terminology will be different or the process may not reflect UK best practice. Therefore you will need to compare local practice with UK practice. For example, in the Damascus airport study referred to at the beginning of this chapter the legislative context was very different. A democratic and open development process similar to the UK planning procedures, which require comprehensive consultation, did not exist. In this case you should highlight the absence of procedures by making comparisons with town planning procedures.

138

Health and safety is another area where, even in the other states of the European Union, local practice may be very different from UK practice.[9]

Planning and development

Most case study projects are considered to be 'development' and require planning permission. The UK system is complex, though, and some small residential projects, for example, may not require permission. This book is not a primer on UK planning practice and you will be expected to have researched key points to include here are the *type* of planning application, the pre-application process, and any issues that flow from the procedure that may need to be resolved at a later date. You may also refer to other government departments that need to be consulted – the Environment Agency, for example, or local authority departments such as Highways. Where your project does not require permission you should explain the reasons why. In this way you are still showing knowledge of the requirements – if not the procedures themselves.

The appendices to the study may be a good place to list the documentation submitted to the local authority as part of the application and the planning permission itself.

Heritage

Not all case studies involve heritage issues. Again, UK practice is different although most countries have some form of legislation that controls the preservation of the historic built environment. If the project is affected by local legislation you should discuss this and compare it with the UK system of listed buildings and conservation areas.

Sustainability

It would be unusual not to refer to the impact of sustainability initiatives on your project. This is an opportunity to explain the basic legislation that may affect your project or the conceptual approach of the office and some of the standards that the office and its clients adopt that exceed current legislation.

Building regulations

There is likely to be a strong overlap with sustainability regulations in the UK. Again, you should show that you have a systematic understanding of UK practice and procedures as well as variations relevant to your project. Approved inspectors, specialist consultants employed directly by the Client or the Architect, increasingly take on the compliance aspects of the Building Regulations.

You might also have to consult other local authority departments such as environmental health.

Health and safety

It is essential that you discuss health and safety legislation – or its absence. In the UK the CDM Regulations affect construction projects and will apply to varying degrees depending on the project. It is an integral part of the design development and detailed design processes. You should be able to explain and discuss the duties of each of the relevant stakeholders – employer, designer, principal contractor and other contractors, the role of the HSE and how health and safety is monitored and develops during the project.

This is also an opportunity to mention other aspects of health and safety where relevant – office policy and procedures, for example.

Inclusive design

Accessibility issues may be covered in the section on building regulations and you may cover these issues there but you should also explain the effects of the wider legislation where relevant. Often, adapting buildings to meet current requirements conflicts with other legislation – such as heritage – and this can be an interesting topic for brief discussion.

Adjoining owner rights

This topic may not be relevant to your case study and you should have shown your knowledge of this area of the Criteria elsewhere – typically in your written examinations or coursework assignments.

You are not expected to be an expert but you should be sensitive to the relevant issues and how they affect the project. Typical topics include rights of way, rights to light (especially in larger cities) and restrictive covenants. Party wall procedures may need to be followed. These are usually handled by specialist consultants, whom you may have to approach during the preparatory work for the study.

Part 3 students normally deal with the regulatory issues reasonably well because researching them involves sifting through files that set out timescales and events with relative clarity. Being procedural, they follow set patterns, where one requirement follows another. Problems occur when you are completely detached from the process and may not fully understand the effect of particular requirements (planning conditions, for example) on the project. If your writing seems dry and lacking in any sense of personal engagement, the examiners will pick up on your detachment.

You also need to be aware of events that should have occurred but did not, the difficulty being that they will not be covered in the files! A more innocent reason may be that correspondence with a particular statutory body did occur but it is covered elsewhere. Surprisingly, the CDM Regulations can still be overlooked or mishandled, despite non-compliance being a criminal offence and the publicity surrounding prosecutions. If you fail to address this area you may fail Part 3. Failure to follow the rules can provide fertile ground for comparative analysis and some critical appraisal. You can easily demonstrate your knowledge and application of regulatory issues by showing that they were not fully addressed.

PROCUREMENT, CONTRACT CHOICE AND TENDERING

The two sections discussed above effectively comprise the first half of the case study. The first requiring a knowledge and understanding of how the office operates, together with some in-depth investigation, and the second effectively a paper-based study, the success of which depends on knowing where to look and asking the right questions. This next section, on procurement, contract choice and tendering can be more difficult. In the first instance, the selection methods are not normally governed by any set of regulations. With the exception of most public sector projects[10] it is essentially a private matter of choice, based on a number of factors that you may have discussed earlier in the case study.

The procurement, contract and tendering choices may also be influenced by the preferences of the architect and/or quantity surveyor. You should note that attitudes to procurement and contract choice are influenced by a complex series of factors that go far beyond the rather simplistic idea that three variables are in play: cost, time and quality.

Procurement processes

The procurement strategy options have already been discussed in the context of the client and the architect's appointment. Depending on the type of project it may be appropriate to discuss the actual procurement processes that take place later on. In particular procurement routes may remain fluid until the tendering stage or may change.

Typically, the choice may change from, for example, management contracting to design and build or traditional to design and build. The architect may be novated to the contractor and/or retain a client role. These changes are normally driven by changes in attitudes to risk by the client or cost. Change at this stage will affect the architect's role and responsibilities and have an impact on resourcing, fees and the appointment. On larger more complex projects it may be appropriate to discuss work package procurement or Contractor Design elements.

This need not be an exhaustive account of these changes from a technical point of view and you should try to concentrate on the key issues as they affect the architect, the office and the resourcing of the project.

Contract choice

You should also refer to the type of construction contract chosen for the project. This may be a standard form – with or without amendments – such as one of the JCT SBC family, or it may be a bespoke contract. Remember, though, that even the standard forms contain variants: 'with or without quantities', for example, or significant Contractors Design Portions (CDPs). You should refer to these where appropriate. Remember also that each 'standard form' has a detailed menu of choices within it giving a limited set of options plus appendices where significant elements of the contract are stated, such as liquidated damages.

Tendering

Tendering should follow 'best practice' procedures, either single or two-stage. You may be able to comment on the transparency of the process, the 'spread' of tenders, any comparisons with the cost plan and subsequent 'value engineering' exercises. The line between bona fide tendering and negotiation may also be blurred. On small projects the architect may control the process but, more often, the details will be administered by the cost consultants. Again, you need not be an expert but you should have a critical understanding of the processes, the use of 'best practice' and the direct effect on the architect – abortive work and additional work resulting from a value engineering exercise.

This part of the case study may also be the appropriate point to 'switch' projects if you have decided that the case study will cover different stages of two separate projects.

You also need to be relatively sophisticated in your understanding and analysis. The task of collecting and organising the requisite data is difficult enough as not all architects' offices receive the complete picture. Targeted conversations with other professionals in the project will be very valuable.

POST-MOBILISATION

This is the part of the case study where you may experience the most problems, for a number of reasons. First, the Part 3 and project programmes are not synchronised. Most projects last longer from start to finish than a Part 3 course, with the result that you may not personally experience all of the various project stages. Although you can backtrack through the office files to understand the basis of the appointment, for example, or follow the planning history, it is impossible to write about contract events that either have not yet happened or are at a very early stage.

You should aim to cover the following, although the completion and post-completion phases may not have taken place. A project that is part way through is satisfactory provided that you can discuss the basic contractual processes:

> the role of the architect
> contract administration
> contract events
> completion
> post-completion.

The role of the architect

The sheer scale of a 'traditional' contract or management contract, where the architect is appointed as lead consultant, may result in you seeing only a small part of the bigger picture. The level of involvement becomes more difficult with design and build contracts, especially where the architect responsible for the original design may not be novated to the main contractor for the post-mobilisation phase.

The role of the architect may be unclear. This is a good example of the value of understanding the conventional or traditional role of the architect in standard construction contracts and comparing this with the role in your case study project as a means of explaining the differences in the role and contractual responsibilities. In brief, the architect has two roles when appointed to be the contract administrator in a traditional SBC contract: i) client agent; and ii) independent adjudicator. As agent you will issue instructions on the client's behalf, for example providing detailed information, such as a schedule of finishes or adding work to the contract, such as additional landscaping.

As agent you also inspect the works to make sure that it complies with the contract documentation. As independent adjudicator you will value the works at regular intervals (in effect deciding a routine claim for payment) and decide any claims made by the contractor for additional costs or time. Post-novation, the contractor is your employer and you will lose your previous agency role and duties to the client, for controlling the quality of the works, for example, and you are unlikely to be involved in contract administration. However sometimes you will still be required, under the terms of your appointment, to retain a quality control function – possibly in the capacity of reporting directly to the client – which sits outside the construction contract.

This may appear to present a problem: 'How do you show an understanding of construction contracts as required by the Part 3 Criteria in a hybrid contracting environment?' Here you can employ comparative analysis and in doing so show your critical understanding of the hybrid contract and standard forms.

Contract administration

Some schools of architecture are very prescriptive about this phase of the contract: for example, that it must constitute 50 per cent of the study. However, a different, more flexible approach can be equally valid, provided that you understand the 'dynamics of the contract' – that is, how the contract works during the construction phase. This includes the following:

> how the works start;
> health and safety and other regulatory compliance issues;
> how variations take place and are formalised;
> how contractors are paid;
> how quality is controlled;
> how documents and drawings are used;
> how unforeseen circumstances are dealt with;
> how issues of delay as well as variations to costs are addressed;
> project completion and handover;
> defects and how they are remedied;
> dispute resolution (under the terms of the contract);
> final agreement of costs.

These are all generic questions and processes that apply to any contract. In traditional contract forms these processes are complex but generally clear. Contract administration requires a paper trail which is usually visible and traceable. In larger contracts, such as management contracts, students tend to see a small fragment or a single package. In design and build contracts, depending on the design development that takes place before the contractor is appointed as well as the architect's role, these processes are more opaque and therefore more difficult to understand, but they generally exist. The proliferation of different design and build contracts makes it difficult to generalise.

Specific terms such as 'architect', 'contract administrator', 'interim certificates' and 'instructions' may vary or be omitted altogether, but some form of contract administration takes place.

Not every project in Part 3 case studies covers all these areas; design and build is an example. If you encounter this situation, you need to develop strategies that:

> allow you to investigate and understand these processes;
> re-package or edit this part of the project so that it is manageable as a case study; and
> be sufficiently objective to take an informed critical view.

These strategies might include taking time and effort to discuss the project with other members of the project team. Only with a closer understanding of these processes will you be able to assess the value of the architect in the process.

Contractual events

Sometimes the 'dynamics of the contract' – the way things change and stakeholders react – can best be explained through the selection of a number of events. For example, the discovery of asbestos may have an effect on time and cost. It will also have an impact on health and safety on site and the assessment of risk. Exceptional weather may lead to a claim for an extension of time.

On larger management contracts you can use the work packages themselves to discuss the same contractual events. Problems with quality and performance are likely to have similar effects although they may not involve the same contractual procedures. If you have detailed knowledge of the particular packages you can still show your critical understanding of the contractual processes.

Completion

It is not always essential to follow a project through to completion – but you should check the requirements of your Part 3 provider. However, you should know the common problems and procedures for completion and these are often popular subjects with professional examiners at the interview. Often in design and build contracts you will still be required to carry out some of the quality functions to ensure that the employer's requirements are met.

Post-completion

Again it is not always essential to have experienced the post-completion phase of your case study project but you should be aware of the procedures. In particular, the process of confirming and rectifying defects prior to the issue of the final certificate.

Critical analysis

'Critical analysis' is referred to at various points in this chapter. The case study is more than a 'diary of events' and is not complete without your analysis. Without your systematic and scholarly analysis you will not show the critical understanding requirements of the Part 3 Professional Criteria and the case study is likely to fail. Therefore it is essential that you use your commentary as a platform for demonstrating your detailed knowledge and understanding through your critical analysis of the subject areas.

It is up to you to decide how you approach this essential part of the case study. If you find that writing and commentary and comment come naturally to you then you may be able to 'knit' the two together seamlessly throughout the text. This is not as easy as it sounds and many students prefer to treat the commentary and their analysis separately. This can be done as a section in its own right at the end of the case study and lead to a set of conclusions and recommendations or it can be included at the end of each subject section, as suggested in the 'Case study structure' on p. 117. There are a number of advantages in including your analysis at the end of each section. The analysis can remain targeted on the issues and events in that section and relate to specific Part 3 Professional Criteria. For example your discussion of the architect's appointment will contribute to meeting the requirements of PC2 *'Clients, users and delivery of services'*. Some issues may be complex and are easier to discuss section by section. They may also affect the way the project develops – possibly as a theme. For example, the lack of a written appointment may signal an informality that also affects resourcing, or may indicate a general lack of professionalism that reappears in the administration of the contract. You may also use your analysis as a way of closing the topic before moving on to the next subject area. Your examiners will have to read it before moving on to the next section and the detail of the commentary will still be fresh in their minds.

Comparative analysis

If critical analysis is essential to meeting the requirements of the Part 3 Criteria then you might also ask: 'What is the most effective way of doing this?' One of the best ways of demonstrating your critical understanding of the relevant Professional Criteria is to use the technique of comparative analysis. This has also been referred to at various points in the chapter – in the discussion of 'A most peculiar practice' and 'International projects'.

A simple approach to the problem of discussing events and showing your understanding is to start by drawing three columns: the first can summarise the 'event'; the second can refer to 'best practice' or a suitable 'model'; the third can summarise, in bullet points, your analysis.

The 'appointment' example mentioned in brief above could be analysed as follows:		
Event or commentary	'Best practice'	Analysis
Brief exchange of letters, brief verbal instructions, no formal appointment	ARB Code: 4.4 RIBA Code S-CON 10-A	Verbal instructions do not meet Codes; standard form of Agreement would state scope of services, etc. avoid misunderstandings, manage the client relationship

You can then use this brief comparative analysis as the basis of your discussion and show your critical understanding of part of PC2 *'Clients, users and delivery of services'.* You can see how this form of analysis – which is similar to the 'experiential learning' method discussed in Chapter 2 – through your demonstration of awareness, helps to distance you from poor practice and in the case of international projects also shows your understanding of UK practice.

Conclusions and recommendations

Your conclusions and recommendations are important and it is worth taking the time to consider these carefully. Too often case studies end abruptly without any conclusions. This is the place where you can draw your earlier comments together and possibly discuss a theme or themes that have emerged from the study but which become more significant when viewed as a totality. This is also the place to reflect on your experience, show what you have learnt and to give your carefully considered recommendations for future practice.

A wider perspective

There is a continuing debate among architectural practices, the RIBA and the ARB about the increasing difficulties that students face in gaining sufficient experience for Part 3 and in some cases the relevance of post-mobilisation experience. Most practices specialise in particular areas and this may make it more difficult for you to gain sufficient experience. The position remains that a registered architect could be working in a variety of scenarios and that a member of the public using his or her services must be able to expect them to be competent contract administrators. From an educational as well as a professional standpoint it is worth remembering that the traditional forms of contract are the starting point for any comparative analysis of alternative forms and therefore a thorough understanding of the principles and how they work in practice is very valuable.

Good practice

Finally in this section, some feedback from professional examiners on what they like and dislike should be useful. Their comments all concern presentation. While taking note of these preferences will not necessarily guarantee success, it should reduce negative feedback, especially in the oral examination.

PRESENTATION

> A clear structure: a summary, contents, a consistent structure with clear section headings and conclusions.
> Spelling and grammar: consistent failure to spell words correctly or construct complete sentences tends to undermine the quality of the content and chip away at your professionalism.
> Careful use of photographs and drawings: include photographs or visualisations of the project at the beginning of the study and throughout the text. Avoid inserting drawings at such a scale that they are illegible. Avoid too many technical drawings unless they have a specific reason: an unworkable detail that led to a contractual delay, for example.
> Project programmes: make sure they are legible.
> Pagination: do include pagination. Examiners tend to reference their comments. It is a small point, but omitting page numbers can be very frustrating.

> Landscape or portrait format: examiners tend not to have a preference but landscape has the advantage that text and illustrations or documents can be set next to each other on the same page. However, check with your Part 3 provider – some require A4 portrait. Also, avoid A3 at all costs.
> Footnotes: these are a good way of including detail and therefore demonstrating relevant knowledge without affecting the flow of the text. They also show your ability to edit and order information, distinguishing what is essential from supporting detail.
> References: use references. They demonstrate further reading and, in an academic context, scholarship. They also give authority to the study.
> Appendices: appendices tend to be used like 'comfort blankets' – they give a (false) sense of security. If you include too many, examiners are unable to find their way to the key documents. You should make sure you have carefully checked the documents you want to include as they sometimes include howling errors that originated in the office. A useful device is to reference appendices so that only the relevant documents are included and to include relevant sections of non-standard documents.[11] The appendices are also good places to locate parts of the study that you have written but decided to edit from the main text. Rather than wasting effort and information these sections can be reused as an appendix.
> Length: the word count is a target. If it appears impossible to meet this without compromising the study, seek prior approval before exceeding it. Remember that the ability to present complex information in an accessible manner is an important professional skill.

Some case study myths

The role of the case study should now be clear but it is also important to explain what the case study is *not* as much as what it is and to deflate some of the misconceptions that surround it.

THE CASE STUDY AS BUILDING STUDY

The first point to make is that the case study is *not* a 'building study' in the conventional sense, as seen in the pages of the architectural press. It is not a critique of the product or the architects' output and it does not try to place a building within a particular architectural movement or genre. The product is clearly important but the case study concerns the *processes* that lead to the finished building or project that may, in turn, be reviewed in the architectural press. However, studies often fall into this category. At worst, they relate a factual account of the building and its context: often including a verbatim 'master plan' and briefing documents passed off as the student's own words but too polished and clearly targeting a particular audience (typically the client organisation or the planning authority) to be the student's own work.

A recent example concerned a historic station in a nameless location. The study discussed the original architect, the design style, its age, the type of construction, heritage issues and the conservation challenges that the design team had to face. It also, for completeness, included actual and projected passenger numbers before and after the project, the number of locomotives operated by the railway companies using the station, the number of employees and the companies' annual turnovers. It was illustrated by some well-chosen historical prints and some typical before-and-after interiors. Ample satellite photos showed the city and the station's location, together with a map of the railway network. Unfortunately, the study did not reach a passing standard and the student was recommended to start again from scratch with a new project.

Case studies like these are frequently dry, factual accounts that borrow heavily, if not directly, from readily available office sources and confuse product and process, primarily at the early stages of the project. When an examiner reads the study, he or she invariably notes that the student also appears detached from the process, as if by absorbing and rehashing the contents of the office records their knowledge alone will be sufficient to pass Part 3. It will not, and professional examiners, with experience of many studies, will not be convinced.

THE POSTGRADUATE DISSERTATION

The case study is *not* a postgraduate dissertation. This may seem surprising as it frequently feels like one and can be about the same length. It also requires a similar amount of effort. However, the case study does not follow the normal academic process of asking a question or posing a hypothesis, exploring the known subject area in depth (and possibly conducting some independent primary research such as an analysis of a particular aspect of JCT contracts), discussing the outcomes and arriving at a set of conclusions, recommendations and pointers for further research. This would be a valuable Master's level dissertation but it is not a Part 3 case study. You should avoid drawing wide, general conclusions from your *particular project* despite your own enthusiasm for the subject.

THE BIGGEST MYTH

The biggest common myth is that the case study has to take as its subject a conventional JCT agreement with the architect as lead consultant, follow it through all the RIBA Work Stages and conclude with the resolution of the final account.

The mythical project normally takes the following form:

1. The project is the extension to a family house in a conservation area on the outskirts of Anytown. The clients (there are always two) are well known to the office and are reliable. The purpose of the project is to upgrade their spacious Edwardian semi-detached villa to accommodate an elderly relative. They have a budget of £350,000.
2. The project falls into the lap of the Part 3 architectural assistant who has just joined the office.
3. A small design team is appointed, including a quantity surveyor, structural engineer and party wall surveyor.
4. The brief is taken (over a cosy chat) at their house and the outline design is agreed without too much discussion. Following consultation, the planning officers welcome the scheme as being in keeping with known planning objectives. (The Part 3 student is congratulated for her/his sensitive design.) The project naturally receives the necessary consents within the statutory period. In the meantime, thorny party wall problems are resolved with adjoining owners. None of these negotiations delay the project.
5. The clients also agree with the architectural assistant's recommendation to employ a single-stage selective tendering process and also with the decision to select the JCT Intermediate Contract 11 as the chosen contract for the project. The quantity surveyor, unusually, also agrees (but might have suggested MW11).
6. The tenders are generally within the budget target. The quantity surveyor prepares a post-tender report.
7. A well-regarded main contractor is chosen for a 20-week programme and the contract proceeds reasonably well. There are a few unforeseen problems below ground which the structural engineer resolves quickly. Revised drawings are issued under the architect's instruction. The client makes some limited changes to the design. The flue to the Aga in the kitchen (a late instruction) proves difficult to route through the roof. An extension of time is agreed.
8. The project reaches practical completion, the defects liability period starts and the draft final account is agreed within two months. All this magically falls within the timescale for Part 3. The architectural assistant remains the 'job runner' throughout, under the watchful eye of one of the partners. All relevant RIBA Work Stages are covered.

As can been seen from the above commentary, the likelihood of a project falling within the Part 3 case study cycle is very remote. Also, students with the ideal, mythical study can still fail to succeed in this part of the Part 3 examination for any of the reasons previously discussed.

You should be aware that these problems are discussed almost every day by academics and practitioners running Part 3 courses. Because Part 3 in general and the case study in particular take a series of 'snapshots' of architectural practice, the problems of gaining the right experience at the right time for students as well as the complex nature of the contemporary environment in which we practice architecture are the topics most frequently discussed by professional examiners when they meet.

Conclusions

Having reached the end of this chapter you should be able to start to write the case study with increased confidence. As an exercise in 'reflection' you might consider how successful it has been in achieving this objective.

> Did it cover all the points you wanted it to cover?
> Was it easy to read?
> Was the structure easy to follow?
> Was it relevant?
> Was it too long?

These are the sort of questions that examiners will ask themselves when reading your case study.

THE ORAL EXAMINATION
CHAPTER 5

This chapter focuses on the oral examination in Part 3 and aims to:

> *explain its purpose;*
> *give a national overview of the range of formats;*
> *indicate what to expect from the examination and how to prepare fully for it; and*
> *discuss the strategies for answering different types of questions and how to avoid pitfalls.*

It also aims to explain the interview from the 'other side of the table', from the professional examiner's point of view: how they make use of the material that you have already prepared for Part 3, the different styles they use and the strategies they adopt.

Schools of architecture use different terminology at different times. For clarity and simplicity I will use the term 'interview' to mean the 'Part 3 oral examination' or, as it is less frequently known, the 'viva voce'. In practice, the three terms are broadly interchangeable. By the end of this chapter you should be better prepared for the experience and, perhaps more importantly, you should understand the value of the exercise and the importance of doing well in it.

The role of the interview

To some professional examiners the interview *is* the Part 3 examination. Of course, strictly speaking, those examiners are not correct, but what they are trying to stress is the importance of the interview in the overall examination and the fact that you cannot pass Part 3 on paper alone – there has to be a face-to-face assessment. And the key to success in the interview can be summarised in three words: 'preparation, preparation and preparation'. The key objective of this chapter is to help you prepare effectively for this essential element of the Part 3 assessment.

'Why use an interview format?'

The answer is potentially very complex but, fundamentally, it is for the same reasons that you are never offered a job in an architectural practice on the strength of your portfolio alone. An interview tests something that is not available in your portfolio. In a job situation this could be as basic as establishing whether your career aspirations fit the available job function. But employers are also trying to see if your ability to think on your feet and to communicate aligns with your talents as evidenced by your design work and other drawings. Even at interview immediately post-Part 2, employers are looking at you as a complete person, wanting to hear evidence of how you have synthesised your previous experience and technical knowledge, weighing up your current design skills and assessing whether you have the potential to make a professional contribution to their office.

The interview is a tried and tested method of assessment. Even in professions that appear entirely skill-based, such as a commercial airline pilot, interviews are an essential part of the selection process. The same has been true throughout history. For example, in the British Navy in the 18th century, recruitment from the upper classes could not provide the required number of officers. Promotion was therefore based on competence and merit. Regardless of social connections, all officers began their careers as ratings. The regulations required a candidate for a commission to pass an oral examination in seamanship after six years' service at sea, including what in today's jargon would be termed 'work-based learning' in key knowledge and skills. In the 18th century, just as today, sound theoretical knowledge was important. Navigation, for example, depended on theoretical models and their application. In the days before longitude this was a highly technical matter. Lunar tables were used to interpret position as well as mental 'dead reckoning'. Practice management – as we might call it today – required mastery of rules and regulations as well as communication skills. Knowledge, professional training, practical experience and competence were infinitely more important than social connections in commanding a fast-moving, close-knit team. These practical abilities, all of which were assessed by oral examination, marked the Navy out from other professions. Professional standards and competence had to be set and maintained, if only to ensure the safety of the ship, its cargo and its crew.

Parallels obviously exist between the 18th-century Navy and 21st-century architectural practice and the idea that professional judgement can only be tested fully at interview is as true today as it was then.[1] Hopefully this example demonstrates that the interview has a particular value beyond the assessment of written material. The core functions of an effective interview are to test possession of specialist knowledge and the application of that knowledge in a practical setting and to elicit a display of reflection and professional judgement when faced with real problems drawn from your experience and/or imaginary scenarios. When answering questions on hypothetical scenarios, you are applying your knowledge to consider a particular problem and speculate on the correct answer. This may appear artificial, but architects do this in a professional and design context continuously. Part of the design process is a series of 'What if ...?' scenarios that require speculation and sometimes tough problem-solving. The difference in the Part 3 interview is that it is more explicit and focused.

In some schools of architecture professional examiners assess written examinations and coursework. Other schools mark the examination scripts and coursework before they are given to the professional examiners. In both systems the examiners are using the complete submission for a number of purposes in the interview. These include the following:

> Confirming
> Exploring
> Reflecting
> Probing
> Filling gaps
> Resolving inconsistencies
> Testing

This range covers 'higher level', more open questioning, through to the 'lower level' activities of testing knowledge with targeted questions. The interview will not follow one exclusive line but will mix approaches so you can expect to discuss issues raised in the case study, for example, in general terms as well as targeted questions that are designed to reassure examiners that you have adequate professional knowledge and understanding of the subject areas covered in the Part 3 Criteria.

The first three, 'confirming', 'exploring' and 'reflecting' can take the form of a conversation with the two examiners that give you the opportunity to expand on issues in your case study or in your career appraisal. One of the key functions of the interview is to show your professional skills and your ability to reflect on your experiential learning and professional development, in particular. Examiners may 'probe' what you have written – or possibly some of your answers – digging a little deeper to test your knowledge or to prompt you to explain something in more detail.

The 'filling gaps' function of the interview can take a variety of forms, such as addressing shortcomings in your PEDRs or, more likely, gaps in your knowledge exposed in your examination scripts and other coursework through to gaps in the case study.

The written examinations are fairly blunt instruments that test a limited range of the required Criteria. They are good at testing legal, contractual and professional knowledge, and certain skills such as the ability to write clearly and with relevance and to 'unpick' a problem under pressure. However, they cannot accurately assess your ability to reflect on experience or your professional judgement. There is a distinction between purely procedural, knowledge-based questions and the problem-based questions that use a core knowledge and apply it to a practical problem. In the former there is a 'right and wrong answer', in the latter there will be a range of answers, some more right than others (depending on the context), and the robustness and completeness of the process by which you arrive at an answer is as important as the result or conclusion. In practical terms, most written examinations provide a limited choice of questions and the pass mark is normally 50 per cent.

The case study builds on professional knowledge, concentrating on how it is applied in a 'real life' practice setting. Its format allows you to deal with issues at a greater level of practical detail. As discussed in Chapter 4, the case study tests your ability to critically analyse complex professional issues using both limited professional experience and relevant knowledge of professional norms. The case study is therefore more multi-faceted than a written examination. It sets down on paper a set of core experiences and makes relevant conclusions. It provides an opportunity to push all the Part 3 buttons, taking in the legal, professional, managerial and contractual issues as it progresses.

The PEDR, at a basic level, is a record of the required relevant practical experience and shows the profession that you have met those requirements. It encourages reflective skills through an assessment of your progress in architectural practice, but examiners can only see evidence of the *range* of experience and cannot easily discern the *quality* of that experience, nor can they accurately assess what you actually learned in the workplace. The career appraisal may help in this respect but it cannot be comprehensive. Its format, an overview, must by its nature be relatively superficial and it will not analyse professional issues in depth. However it show how you meet the Criteria through your professional development.

The 'answering inconsistencies' function is closely linked to filling the gaps. For example, there may be inconsistencies between what is recorded in your PEDR and what you discuss in your career appraisal. Some of your written examination answers may be flawed or inconsistent, betraying obvious and possibly fundamental errors. Parts of the case study may be weak or, at worst, missing.

However, the main function of the interview is to bring these elements together to test your professional judgement by discussing professional issues that you can relate directly to your experience. Because you are unlikely to have had much professional experience, examiners may pose hypothetical questions that take you beyond your experience but remain within the boundaries of an acceptable level of professional knowledge at the Part 3 stage.

It is important to repeat that they are also testing your reflective skills: the key distinguishing characteristic of the 'thinking professional', demonstrating an ability to weigh up often conflicting and sometimes dissonant factors to arrive at a rational conclusion that is reasonably secure. In this way the interview goes beyond the purely technical skills and knowledge of a competent, experienced architectural assistant to reveal the reflective skills that clients and other members of the design team value.

Format of the interview

The interview format is relatively straightforward. Although there is a broad range of Part 3 courses in the UK, different types of course delivery from 'beginner' to 'refresher' and a mix of different examination methods, the interview format is consistent. The variations occur in the details that examiners are being asked to assess.

Each interview is conducted by two professional examiners. Under the revised RIBA Part 3 Regulations, each examiner will have been given a copy of the different parts of the candidate's written submission: the PEDR, curriculum vitae, career appraisal, case study, examination scripts and/or assignments (or will have access to them). Examiners split the workload but may share parts. For example, some schools ask both examiners to mark everything: the written examination scripts, case study, etc. Other schools mark the material in house and ask the professional examiners to second-mark the material. Certain schools may ask for examiner comments only and invite examiners to use the material as the basis for the interview, choosing subjects with which the candidate is familiar. In any event, you must pass all parts of the examination including the all-important interview.

You should be clear before the interview about how your work has been assessed and how the workload is likely to have been allocated between examiners. This is vitally important as in some schools a provisional borderline fail in the written examinations may be moderated to a pass on the basis of interview performance. (It is very unlikely to operate in the reverse sense.) However, examiners will only have limited discretion here. You should be aware of your weaker areas from your experience in the written examinations. To rescue the situation you must thoroughly prepare answers for all the examination questions (not just the ones you attempted) and give a sparkling performance at the interview.

The time allocated for the examiners to conduct the interview and to reflect on your performance is likely to be one hour and examiners should not see more than the maximum of six candidates per day recommended by the RIBA. They will have been sent a large bundle of material approximately four weeks in advance to give them time to read the submissions and confer over concerns and queries. Interviews frequently run late for a variety of reasons but examiners try not to overrun on the understanding that to do so can be to your disadvantage as much as your advantage.

The way the interview is conducted varies but generally examiners recognise that candidates will be nervous. Their aim in the first few minutes is to try to put you at your ease, typically by opening a conversation about what project you are currently working on.

The interview may have four distinct phases:

1. The first phase discusses your current experience, the content of the career appraisal and PEDR and any interesting events in your career to date.
2. The second phase might look at your case study. This will be conducted by one examiner.
3. The third phase might then ask you questions about the examination scripts or any other material that forms part of your written submission.
4. Finally, examiners will generally round off with some questioning on topical issues and ask if there is anything that you would like to add. For example: 'Was there something that we have missed that you would like to talk about?'

Different schools vary the format depending on the in-house assessment regime. The key point to remember is that examiners are using the material available in a variety of ways to help you to perform at your best. This sometimes means that they may ask relevant but hypothetical questions to probe areas not covered elsewhere. These topics are expanded on below in the section on preparing for the interview.

Finally, for completeness, it is worth adding that each examination centre will operate some form of quality assurance system to meet university or institutional requirements and professional requirements. This involves the appointment of external examiners (who may also have a background as professional examiners but will not examine candidates at the institution that appointed them) to review the examination process. In this way all written work and the interviews are sampled. Candidates are normally warned if an external examiner is likely to sit in on the interview. His or her presence should have no significance for the candidate: the external examiner works within strict guidelines that require him or her to examine the *process* and not the individual student. External examiners then write a report to the institution (usually for the Academic Registrar) rather than the school of architecture, commenting on the conduct and fairness of all aspects of the examination, including the interview and commenting on the parity, or otherwise, with standards elsewhere. They will also be required to confirm – or not, depending on the quantity of the comments – if all the ARB/RIBA Criteria have been met. External examiner reports are therefore an essential part of the quality assurance process. The reports are often published on university websites. Both the ARB and the RIBA pay particular interest to the comments made by external examiners, both in terms of any observed shortcomings and the evidence of 'best practice'. Their reports are passed down to the school for comment and action, if appropriate. The external examiners' reports also form an important part of the regular submissions made by each school of architecture to the RIBA and the ARB.

'Where do examiners come from?'

The RIBA maintains a list of professional examiners as a way of ensuring that candidates are examined to a similar standard across the UK. The list holds the details of registered and chartered architects who are also generally in practice or who mix teaching professional and management studies with architectural practice. Professional examiners must have a minimum of five years in full-time architectural practice and attend the RIBA induction and training sessions organised by Part 3 providers and the RIBA Education Department. They tend to be established practitioners with an interest in professional issues and might be a visiting lecturer on professional studies topics included in the Professional Criteria. Schools and examination centres are asked to appoint at least one of the pair of examiners from the RIBA list and all examiners are encouraged to examine at more than one location. This still allows the schools of architecture (and other Part 3 providers) a large degree of autonomy in the way they deliver Part 3 and their choice of examiners. This flexibility is encouraged not only by the schools, which can shape the delivery of the course to suit university resources, but also by students who can access the most appropriate course for their particular needs. Examiners gain a wider experience of practice and assessment regimes and also contribute by sharing 'best practice' through participation in formal examiner meetings. The time examiners spend on Part 3 can count towards their annual CPD requirement and, indeed, examiners often remark on the 'instant CPD' experience of examining: it allows them to see a range of architectural practice and project administration and to reflect on different approaches and 'best practice' – especially in the light of some of the doubtful practices discussed in Chapter 4.

You will see that professional examiners must have an interest in the education of young architectural professionals in order to sustain the effort required to read all the material required for the interview, to consider the appropriate line and content of questioning and to arrive at a professional judgement concerning the candidate's competence to practise. They are committed to the process. They are experienced – but not necessarily in every field. They may be experts, but they will mould their questions to the more moderate requirements of Part 3.

'What benchmarks do examiners use?'

Examiners are experienced professionals and not academics. However, external examiners report that they all generally examine to the same standard and are fair in the conduct of the interview regardless of the candidates' backgrounds. Examiners will work to a set of Criteria which should be published in the course handbook provided to you when you started your Part 3 course. The assessment criteria will be set to align with national standards at an appropriate level. Part 3 is considered to be at 'Master's-level' (sometimes indicated as level 7).[2]

Examiners are looking for a competent professional who meets the Professional Criteria. This does not mean that students must exceed the professional requirements, although many do. Examiners are therefore looking for:

> awareness of relevant issues;
> an appropriate level of professional knowledge;
> professional judgement;
> the ability to reflect on performance and experience.

You are not expected to know everything or be able to recite conditions from your professional appointment or JCT clauses. (This can be a dangerous strategy as details change daily and relying on your memory inevitably means that what you recall is at best incomplete and at worst out of date.)

With borderline candidates the professional examiner is obliged to maintain professional standards and consider the 'public interest' as well as, in some cases, protecting candidates from potentially putting themselves in a professional setting in which they will not cope. Unlike the university assessor who may be able to moderate a fail to a pass on a number of prescribed grounds, the examiner does not have this luxury. If there is sufficient doubt about your knowledge, competence, experience or judgement, you will not pass.

'Why do interviews seem to vary?'

Interviews are tailored to the candidate. Examiners prepare for the interview by considering all the material that you have provided, arriving at an independent view of your abilities, gaps in your knowledge and experience and any doubts about your critical and evaluative skills. Examiners will then confer before the interview and exchange notes. They will very often have arrived at the same view about your knowledge and competence independently – but not always. Through discussion, and possibly by raising queries with the course leader, they will develop a strategy for each *individual* interview, designed around the candidate's perceived strengths and weaknesses.

Typical questions and strategies for answering them

The following sections set out the likely progress of the interview and the types of question that may be asked together with some guidance on suitable strategies to answer those questions. Examiners will normally split the workload: one looking at examination papers, coursework and experience, the other concentrating on the case study. They will both have read your career appraisal and will have discussed this together with the other parts of your submission.

Questions fall into the following categories, in order of increasing complexity.

QUESTIONS OF FACT

These are factual questions to do with your experience or the case study. A few examples might be:

> 'What were you doing between February and August this year?'
> (Detailed design work or production information?)
> 'Did you follow a single or two-stage tender process?'

These are very 'closed' questions. You are being asked to fill gaps in your experience or knowledge or in the material you have presented. A simple factual answer is all that is required to satisfy the examiner. If satisfied by your answers he or she will then move on.

Difficulties occur when these essentially simple questions are not answered fully; they begin to raise doubts.

You might also be questioned on areas that you should know about but which are beyond your experience. With the growing diversity of architectural practice, these questions are increasingly important.

QUESTIONS ABOUT CORE KNOWLEDGE

These cover essential core knowledge not evidenced or answered adequately in the documentary submissions. They could utilise material from the case study or the written examinations. An example might be:

> 'You seem to have avoided any mention of the CDM Regulations. Can you tell me about Designer duties?'

This is a fairly 'closed' question. There is only one answer but with a range of detail. Again, you are filling apparent gaps in your knowledge.

A more 'open' question but with a similar 'right or wrong' answer format might be:

> 'Can you explain how the office applied for town planning permission for the project?'

Here the examiner is looking for a fairly specific answer to do with the different ways of applying for consent. There is a limited range of answers which you need to know, together with the reasons for the method selected.

A more 'open' question could take you beyond your immediate experience but still be firmly within examination territory. It could take the scenario from an examination question:

> 'Looking at the scenario, what are the town planning issues that may affect the advice you might give a client?'

This is a fairly speculative question but the examiner is looking for both your basic knowledge and an element of judgement in selecting and applying that knowledge. The answer would start with a short discussion of the issues, touch on the documents you would refer to and who you would speak to. For example, a redundant industrial building with the potential to be turned into a mix of social housing and loft apartments will, following reference to the appropriate sources of information, require an appropriate type of planning application depending on various relevant factors. (Your answer will need to be detailed, specifying which sources and their effect on the type of application.) With this type of open question, examiners are looking at how you arrive at the answer and how you think around the problem. They may give you the opportunity to correct yourself by asking a subsidiary 'closed' question such as:

> 'Can you explain the reasons for making a full planning application for this building?'

Here they are probing for an important detail. In this case the project involves a 'change of use'; therefore it will require a full planning application. Getting the answer wrong will not automatically mean that you fail but it will make the examiners begin to question your core professional knowledge.

QUESTIONS ABOUT THE SUBSTANCE OF THE CASE STUDY

These may include genuine queries about events, often as a result of a point not being explained sufficiently clearly in the case study. For example, a simple 'closed' factual question:

> 'Were you employed to carry out the dimensional survey that caused so many problems later in the project?'

A secondary, more 'open' question might flow from this:

> 'What issues might you be concerned about, given the contractual relationship with your client?'

This has a number of facets. There are potential issues about duty of care and breach of contract. You would be expected to pick up on the word 'contractual' and the implied invitation to discuss general issues about complying with the terms of your appointment. You would also be expected to pick up on the implication that you might have breached a term of your contract and be open to a claim. You should be going through a series of questions in your mind. A dimensional survey is not a 'normal' service under the RIBA Standard Agreement. As an additional service, was it recorded as such? If not, why did we do it? Negligence may be relevant. A very good answer might discuss the type of claim and the remedies available.

A third question on the same topic might be:

> 'Are there any other issues outside the contractual relationship that might concern you?'

Suddenly the line of questioning is much more 'open'. The key point here is to think beyond the architect's appointment. The main area to address, especially concerning the client–architect relationship, is to do with Standards and Codes of Conduct. Was the architect competent to carry out the survey? Did he or she have the necessary skills or resources? If the Part 3 student undertook the survey was he or she adequately supervised? A fairly small-scale problem can lead to a complex range of issues.

Similar questions can arise when an architect has given advice that is beyond his or her competence and which is not referred to in their appointment, for example giving commercial advice on capital values or returns.

You will see that these questions can unravel like a ball of string. The examiner is probing your knowledge and your ability to think around a professional problem. The sub-questions are there to help rather than confuse you. The examiner is also looking at your sense of professional judgement based on reflection. For example:

> 'On the basis of the events that occurred, would you do this again or would you handle the situation differently?'

QUESTIONS ABOUT INCONSISTENCIES

These address areas that have raised a doubt in the examiner's mind. This often occurs when two statements are contradictory, when you say the wrong thing to make the right point or when you have arrived at the right answer but by a tortuous path.

> 'You write here that you used a Building Notice but that you later had discussions with the Fire Officer. Can you explain what happened?'

This could be a simple error and the examiner is giving you the opportunity to correct it. Be honest and say you made a mistake and made a full plans application. That might be enough: a simple answer that corrects the inconsistency.

A secondary question might be:

> 'Why is this important?'

This question is more open. The examiner is interested to know if you are aware of the significance of the error.[3] These questions are essentially to do with your knowledge but involve a level of judgement too.

QUESTIONS THAT TEST YOUR REFLECTIVE SKILLS AND JUDGEMENT

The interview is the only place where these aspects of your development can be tested realistically. These questions fall into two sub-categories:

1. Questions that ask you to reflect on your professional development through discussion of events in your professional experience or the case study.
2. Questions that take you beyond your immediate experience.

In the first category you are showing self-awareness and reflective skills that allow you to reach a conclusion. In the second category you are working where all architects have to work at least some of the time: at the limits of your knowledge, with limited information and in a new situation.

Questions in the first sub-category might be:

> 'What do you think about the use of the JCT Intermediate Contract (IC11) for this project?'

If your answer is, 'We always use the Intermediate Contract. It's short and the office is familiar with it', you may very well fail!

The question (which could be about any type of contract) is asking you to reflect on the choice. It is asking you to think about its appropriateness based on the published 'best practice' guidelines. In the Intermediate Contract example you could say that the office always uses it but that this practice has its own dangers and go on to outline what those dangers are. However, you might also conclude that the IC11 form is too complex, again giving your reasons. On balance, you should apply 'best practice'.

Another question might be:

> 'How were the latter stages of the works handled?'

Your answer would consider the run-up to practical completion and the process of contract administration, or the handling of the information flow and how possible delays were dealt with. Again, the examiner is asking you to reflect on the process. One answer could be:

We were being pushed by the client and the contractor to certify practical completion. On balance the building was not complete in our opinion and there may have been health and safety issues post-occupation. We were very fortunate that it ran as smoothly as it did. If I were doing it again, I would try to explain to the client the implications of handing the building over before it is complete. He could make his own mind up and choose to take possession or wait until the building was, in our opinion, complete.

Questions in the second sub-category might be:

> 'Clients approach your office to design a small extension to their house. They say they worry that it is too small a project for the office but hope that you will agree to do it for them. What would you do?'

There are ethical, Code, Standard, competence, resourcing and insurance issues here. You need to be able to take each issue and address it separately. You also need to be honest about your professional skills at this stage in your career.

Another question might be:

> 'The contractor calls you and says there is a problem with a particular product or component that you have specified. What do you do?'

There is unlikely to be a 'right' answer here. The examiner is aiming to see how you work through the problem. There is little to refer to in terms of 'best practice'. The question can apply to any contract or any role. The instinct is to reach for the contract in a conventional setting but really the answer is pragmatic as well as contractual – 'Is the contractor right?' Check the specification. Does the product on site correspond with what was specified? Visit the site and check, having done your research. Is there a simple way of resolving the problem? Can the product be sent back? Is there a cost and/or time implication? If so, who do you inform and what is your decision? If all else fails, *in extremis*, notify your professional indemnity insurer, flagging up an early warning of a possible claim. You will also need to be able to explain what you can do under the terms of the contract. This shows your awareness of professional issues as well as contractual ones.

QUESTIONS ABOUT GENERAL AND TOPICAL ISSUES THAT CONCERN THE PROFESSION

These will include questions about recent changes in legislation, typically town planning, CDM and the Building Regulations, and general questions about procurement and the role of the architect. In order to keep up to date you should read the practice and management, planning and legal pages of the professional journals, especially in the run-up to the interview. Remember, your examiners will be reading the same articles and will be interested in the same topics.

Finally, and you need to have prepared a good answer to this one:

> 'What are you planning to do after Part 3?'

IN SUMMARY

The interview varies from any other form of assessment in its dynamic quality: within certain limits it can go almost anywhere. However, you should be clear about the hierarchy of questions:

1. Factual: basic knowledge required by the ARB and the RIBA.
2. Omissions and errors: covering perceived gaps in your basic knowledge.
3. Queries in your work: addressing simple misunderstandings and inconsistencies.
4. Reflection: on your experience.
5. Judgement: critical analysis of scenario-based or real problems.
6. The profession: evidence of topical reading and engagement with the post-Part 3 requirements of CPD.

The way in which examiners arrive at their interview strategy is generally consistent. Both examiners will initially look at your professional experience: have you worked for the minimum period in architectural practice? What is your range of experience? Are there any gaps or inconsistencies? The CV is there as a brief summary of the facts and is unlikely to prompt any questions but examiners will use it to note previous achievements, contributions to exhibitions and publications and also to see how you gained Parts 1 and 2, whether by a conventional architectural education or through the RIBA Examination for Office-based Candidates or the ARB Prescribed Examinations. They will both read the career appraisal and note your degree of critical self-awareness through your reflective commentary as well as your career progression.

Preparing for the interview

REVIEWING YOUR CV, PEDR AND CAREER APPRAISAL

Major inconsistencies in your written submissions can have a negative effect on the interview. Because the examiners will be doing so, it is important that you also read your CV, career appraisal and PEDR together to spot any inconsistencies. If there are any, prepare a convincing explanation for them. A poor answer to a simple question about your experience which shows a lack of self-awareness or preparedness, tries to cover your tracks or play down the error as being immaterial will immediately begin to undermine your professionalism and credibility. A straightforward, factual question can potentially stir up doubts in the examiner's mind about you and colour his or her subsequent questions. This is not a reason to fail in itself, but within the dynamics of the interview it can turn a positive position into a neutral or even a negative one.

REVIEWING THE WRITTEN EXAMINATION SCRIPTS

This can be a nerve-racking process for candidates. As a minimum, make sure that you have reviewed the question papers. Unfortunately some students fail to do this, thereby immediately undermining their credibility. It is important to review your papers to demonstrate the qualities expected of a professional: reflection and judgement. This is especially true if as a consequence of this review procedure you come to a different and more mature conclusion. This impresses the examiners at a practical level too, showing that you are conscientious and committed to giving the best possible performance. Be prepared to add to the answers that you have already given during the written examinations and also to answer those that you did not attempt.

You should start by evaluating your examination performance – not immediately after the exams but some time later, as a calm, measured review with your study group or your office. Prepare new answers. If you misunderstood the question, now is the time to correct it. If you made a mistake then note the correct answer. In a scenario question, think around the possible solutions in the knowledge that there is unlikely to be a single correct answer.

REVIEWING THE CASE STUDY

Re-read your case study and assess it honestly. It may have been a rushed submission. Spelling and grammatical errors may not have been corrected. You may have left something out. You will have at least four weeks to correct these and any other mistakes. Use this time wisely. Discuss particular points with other Part 3 students or your mentor in the office. Take this opportunity to look at your critical analysis and refine it. You will see that the process is essentially reflective again. Examiners will appreciate the effort, but more importantly you are demonstrating an essential professional skill, showing that you are revisiting different areas, recognising potential aspects for improvement and acting accordingly. If this sounds artificial consider it in terms of being a parallel of the design process where we review, change and refine design ideas.

Like the design process, changing your mind or refining your position are strengths not weaknesses. Examiners will take this into account in their overall judgement of your written submission and performance at the interview. Answer questions as succinctly as possible and try not to drift into different or related topics where you may not be so sure of your answers.

The end of the interview

If time permits, both examiners will be interested in asking you about topical professional issues. This reveals your level of interest in the profession and preparation for post-Part 3 CPD. They will also ask you if there is anything that you would like to ask them or add that has not been covered in the interview. They will not be able to tell you whether you have passed or failed: that will be decided at a meeting of all examiners at the end of the complete examination process.

Key points about the interview

By this stage you should have concluded that the only way to ready yourself for the interview is to prepare and then prepare again. Very few Part 3 students can take the interview and pass without adequate preparation. Preparation is in itself a demonstration of professionalism and that crucial professional skill: the ability to reflect.

> *Review all your work dispassionately*   Look back at your PEDR and career appraisal. Remember that the PEDR is a contemporary record. It may not be a completely accurate record of your experience as you may have missed out events or not recognised the significance of a particular event at the time. There may be gaps. Review the career appraisal. Many students rush this and fail to appreciate how the professional examiners use it.
> *Go through your examination papers*   Discuss answers with friends and colleagues.
> *Look again at your case study*   Search for inconsistencies and gaps. Finding gaps is more difficult and again you may need the objective view of a friend or mentor. If this is not available look again at any guidance notes that you were given, or even the guidance in this book.
> *Make an honest evaluation of your strengths and weaknesses*   Read around those areas that you are less familiar with, particularly different forms of contract. Refresh your memory by revisiting the essential building blocks: the Codes and Standards; the standard forms of appointment; published client guidance; and basic legislation: town planning; building regulations; CDM Regulations; and inclusion.
> *Follow up on areas where you lack experience*   If you are not working in a project environment that requires full architectural services, note the ones that you do and do

not provide. Look at the contractual duties of the architect under standard JCT forms of contract and the procedures that you need to follow for variations, valuations and certification.
> *Take some imaginary scenarios* Consider your response and the documentation to which you would refer.
> *Keep up to date* Read the practice and legal pages in the professional journals. These will often give an insight into a situation that you may encounter in the office or at least give you examples of the way to unpick some of these difficult practical problems, making reference to 'best practice' models.

On the day, try to relax. Dress in a way that makes you feel comfortable and that would be appropriate for a client meeting or a job interview. Get there in good time: a breathless, perspiring interviewee will feel at a disadvantage (and might unnerve the examiners!). Finally, remain calm, listen to the questions and try to enjoy the process. The examiners are genuinely trying to help you and they will use their skills to put you in a position where you can fill gaps or alleviate doubts and demonstrate your knowledge and professional judgement.

What happens if you fail?

For almost all candidates that fail, it will be the first examination that they have failed in their adult life. Some very capable candidates fail. Apart from the inevitable knock to your confidence, you might feel resentful that other candidates who were not as able or motivated as you did pass. You might blame the system and not your abilities.

Failure in a professional examination is not terminal and is not considered a slur on your abilities. Instead, it is frequently because you have not developed sufficient professional competence, or that you did not prepare thoroughly enough. The examiners are not able to give you the benefit of the doubt because they have to maintain professional standards and protect you from claims and the public from the possibility of inadequate service. Candidates will normally be able to resit within six months. Occasionally examiners will recommend a 12-month period to allow you to gain more relevant or complete experience and to widen and deepen your knowledge to sustain and improve your professional development.

This six- or 12-month period can be a very rich learning opportunity. In the first instance, the pressure to submit all your documentary material is off, although as a matter of good practice you should still complete the PEDR and update your career appraisal to show, in written form, you have continued to develop professionally to the point where you now meet the required standard set by the Part 3 Criteria. To that effect, the commentary and reflection on your professional development as evidenced by your revised career appraisal is very valuable. It shows an awareness of where your weaknesses are and how you have addressed them. It will also act as a prompt to your examiners, direct them to particular topics and help to persuade them that you now meet the required standards to practise at a competent level. If you failed some written examinations, now is the time to re-engage with the subject material. If you need more experience, this will have been flagged up and you will be able to discuss this with your office. The richness of this learning opportunity comes from the reflective process: reviewing experience and your own level of knowledge, professional development and competence. Your school of architecture should debrief you and give you additional guidance. This short break in your professional progression will not affect your career prospects.

Myths and legends

It is worth winding up this chapter by dispelling some of the misinformation that the interview attracts. Nothing seems to create more discussion among students than the interview. Your instinct in preparing for the interview will be to ask around to get a feel for the process and the typical questions that are asked. You will quickly find that the advice varies widely and that newly registered architects' memories are at best selective, and at worst defective when it comes to discussing the experience. Some will have found it straightforward, some very difficult, which will fatally prejudice any anecdotal feedback. It is far safer to rely on briefings from the Part 3 teaching team and far wiser to evaluate your own strengths and prepare around them.

Conclusions

It should now be clear how the interview process works, how each part of your written submission is used in the interview, the format of the interview, the types of question you might be asked, the reasons behind the various lines of questioning and what skills you will need to pass. You should also have gained an insight into the way examiners prepare for the interview and use the materials you have provided for them.

> Do not try to find a formula for the possible content of questions. You will now appreciate that there is a hierarchy of questions – from basic factual questions,

the answers to which will satisfy the examiners that your core knowledge is sufficiently comprehensive, to the more speculative questions that test your judgement. Similarly, do not hang on every detail of the sample questions given above. They are indicators not models. No two candidates will be asked the same questions in the same way!

> If there is one piece of advice that is relevant to the interview and to your professional conduct generally, it is to be very measured and accurate in what you say. An observer of the professions once remarked that it is in the nature of professionals to say less than they know.[4] This is a difficult balancing act at Part 3, where you are trying to show the extent and quality of your knowledge. What it means is that a professional tends to give advice that is relevant to the point in question and nothing else. It is a useful discipline to acquire.

> Finally, to emphasise the point: success in the interview depends on thorough preparation. The examiners will do their utmost to give you the chance to show your knowledge and skills. With this opportunity comes the risk of failing to satisfy the examiners that you are a competent practitioner: not all-knowing but sufficiently aware and professionally cautious to respect your clients' interests and to maintain the standards of the profession as well as contributing to the progress of architecture. Ultimately this is the criterion by which we will all be judged.

One last thought. The interview is a holistic event – it brings together and tests, for the first time, all the different parts of your formal education and experiences that have contributed to your professional development. It is natural therefore that the main aspects of Part 3 have been brought together in the commentary. The commentary has emphasised the need to show your competence through your professional knowledge and your professional skills. In particular, comprehensive preparation, effective communication, using your knowledge to support problem solving and lastly reflection: showing how you have learnt from both your experience and knowledge of 'best practice' to propose new solutions to normal professional problems. This last process of reflection will already be evidenced in your career appraisal and your case study. Its importance can only be restated for, in your future independent career after Part 3, the professional context will be different, new procurement methods will have been developed, new contract clauses will have been devised and new forms of appointment will be used. However, your examiners will be satisfied that even though the problems and context in the future will be different, you will have demonstrated a robust process where you have reflected on your experience – using the professional knowledge available at that snapshot in time, the interview – to reach considered conclusions using 'best practice'.

AFTER PART 3
CHAPTER 6

The purpose of this chapter is to provide guidance on:

> *registration with the ARB;*
> *professional membership of the RIBA;*
> *continuous professional development (CPD);*
> *immediate and medium-term actions to consolidate and advance your professional career;*
> *further professional development;*
> *taking on further responsibility; and*
> *some reflection on the future challenges of a changing profession and how you can prepare to meet them.*

Some of the points made may seem obvious but feedback from students suggests that things do not always run as smoothly as you might wish.

Registration

When you pass Part 3 a number of things happen. Unfortunately, these events are not always immediate. First, you will receive a recognised qualification from the university or other provider in the form of notification that you have passed. The official documentation will follow in the form of a recognised award and this usually takes some time. In order to expedite matters the university or provider will send the official pass list to the ARB and the RIBA. You will not be able to register until the ARB receives official notification. This can be frustrating, but both the university and the ARB are aware of the urgency and will try to deal with the 'baton passing' from institution to institution as quickly as possible. You will need to complete the necessary registration forms and send the appropriate fee. It is important that you confirm your work address. Following registration your name will be entered on the register and will be in the public domain. If you change your office, you must notify the ARB. In order to remain on the register you will need to pay the annual registration fee. Your office may offer to pay the registration fee or you may wish to pay it yourself and declare it on your annual tax return as an allowable expense.

You are now *personally* responsible for meeting the standards of competence and professional conduct set out in the Standards of the ARB Code of Conduct. If you carry out any *pro bono* work, for example for a charity or non-profit-making organisation, or carry out any private work in a personal capacity, you must have appropriate professional indemnity insurance cover and be prepared to maintain it. This may, rightly, make you think twice about taking on private commissions and may seem unfair and harsh as it appears to effectively block one of the traditional routes to setting up your own practice, but it is a statutory rule and breaking it can lead to prosecution by the Professional Conduct Committee of the ARB under the Architects Act 1997. Registered architects are prosecuted and fined on a regular basis. You also do not want to leave yourself personally liable to the risk of facing a claim without insurance. Declaring yourself bankrupt does not help as this step is also in breach of the Code. Similarly, resigning from the register to avoid prosecution will be counter-productive.

Professional membership

The significant majority of registered architects join the RIBA as Chartered members. However, this is not always appropriate – in teaching for example – and some registered architects prefer simply to remain on the register rather than be a member of an organisation that takes on a wider remit: the promotion of architecture. It is not the purpose of this book to promote the RIBA – it is more than capable of doing that itself. However, you will see that it has a great input into architectural education and continuing education in practice. It also offers members a range of services, such as a legal helpline and a low-cost professional indemnity insurance package that covers the low fee or 'no fee' work described above. It is a useful resource for contractual and planning updates and has a strong regional base outside London. Student membership of the RIBA is free. In order to make membership attractive and accessible to recently registered architects, the RIBA has a sliding membership fee scale. Some offices pay for professional membership. This is not entirely altruistic as there is also a requirement that RIBA-registered practices have a percentage of their employed registered architects as RIBA members. This is seen as providing an enhanced quality of client service through access to the RIBA's resources. The RIBA is sometimes dismissed as a club that only serves the interests of its members, but that is unfair – its remit is far wider. The RIBA is also an effective lobbying organisation and can act for architects collectively in a way that individual registered architects would find very difficult. It is a voice for the profession and, as such, it is consulted by other professions, the construction industry and government. It also has an international reputation and presence. Chartered members, through the regional network, also benefit from the extensive networking opportunities and wider possibilities offered by collaborative working with other chartered members.

Continuous Professional Development

In a knowledge-based profession it is essential to keep up to date and in touch with issues that affect the profession. Just when you thought it was all over, it seems unfair to burden you with another long-term educational requirement. The ARB and RIBA Codes make it explicit that you must be competent to practise. To remain competent also requires keeping up to date and you should allocate time to this. You may have completed a Personal Development Plan as part of your preparations for Part 3 and the new Criteria require you to consider future practice. The RIBA has gone a step further by making CPD mandatory. It has agreed a core syllabus that members must follow. You now record CPD online via the members' section of the RIBA website. A minimum of 35 hours per year is required. The RIBA takes this seriously and polices members' participation.

You will already be aware from the events organised by your practice that CPD enjoys a wide definition. Beyond the strict requirement to remain competent, a number of manufacturers and other providers see RIBA-approved CPD as a fair commercial opportunity to inform members about their products and services. CDM and health and safety legislation and practice also represent a significant RIBA CPD requirement. The full RIBA CPD syllabus is listed in Appendix 6. Reading this book, post-registration, probably meets some CPD requirements. Closer to home, studio teaching, participating in interim and final design crits, giving lectures and acting as a professional examiner all count towards some of your CPD time.

Further professional development

Human resources specialists are quick to state that we will all have three to four careers during our working lives. This sounds extreme, especially in relation to the professions with their high barriers to entry and recognised specialisms. However, you will already have experienced the diversity of careers within the architectural profession, from teachers to specialists, for example those working in 'heritage' which requires an additional set of skills. Inevitably, this calls for further study, and universities deliver a range of specialist courses covering a wide range of subjects. Some architects choose to combine architecture with another specialism such as construction law and may go even further and become construction barristers. Ironically, in any learning environment, although you might be studying another subject you should remain aware of the special skills and holistic way of thinking that is part of an architect's training.

Taking on further responsibility

Part 3 students are highly motivated and develop a range of professional skills, including working under pressure, prioritisation of resources and time management, communication and presentation skills – not forgetting reflective and evaluative skills. Your ambitions will initially be focused on becoming qualified and registered, but within a relatively short period of time your competence will reach a level where you will be keen to take on more responsibility at project and possibly managerial level. If there is a hierarchy in architecture it is a fairly flat and broad one. There is also a fluidity and movement within the profession that comes from the mutual recognition of its skills. The external recognition of your competence by the public in general and clients in particular results in opportunities to start new practices. Although our training makes us 'risk averse', the architectural profession and the construction industry provides opportunities for entrepreneurship. The high barriers to entry make it more difficult for other professionals to compete and the relatively low capital and start-up costs make starting a practice relatively easy, especially with a supportive set of nascent clients to lubricate the cash flow. At this point the professional resources offered by the RIBA are invaluable. You may not earn as much as other professionals but you will enjoy respect and the sense of achievement that comes from creating and adding to the built environment. For the first time, you will be in control of your own professional destiny.

The changing profession

There is a cliché that architecture is a learning profession rather than a learned profession. Unlike some professionals who are relatively insulated from change, either by their legal responsibilities to others (such as lawyers and accountants) or the stability of the client and user framework (as in the medical profession where there is effectively only one client), the architectural profession is an integral part of the construction industry. This has its downside in times of recession. The profession is also directly affected by structural changes in the industry as well as the questioning of the status of professionals in general. The traditional position of the architect as a bridge between demand (the client) and supply (the construction industry) only continues to exist seamlessly on relatively small projects. The architect's status as the independent arbitrator of contractual disputes, while still acting as the client's agent, has been difficult to maintain either theoretically or in practice. Different methods of procurement and partnering arrangements all affect the way architects work as members of the professional construction team.

The architectural profession is made up of a range of practice types. Traditionally, the sole practitioner has been the model or benchmark for Part 3 and the profession as a whole. Small practices continue to thrive despite forecasts of their demise. It is impossible to generalise about the type and size of commissions carried out by small practices. Also, small projects are not simple and may share the construction complexities of much larger projects. Working for owner-occupiers on difficult residential projects covers the full range of skills that an architect requires to practise effectively and, no doubt, others besides. Heritage work calls for a different and complementary knowledge base. Projects for end-user professional and institutional clients call for specialist briefing and management skills. The knowledge and skills required for hospitals and sports stadia are not interchangeable. In response to these different requirements, and also the interests of different parts of the profession, specialist practices have emerged to fill particular niches. The profession may restructure itself to make these specialist niches more explicit in the same way that the medical and legal professions have done. The RIBA, as well as a number of specialist providers, deliver courses and organise CPD events in response to changes in the profession – from conservation to BIM.

Looking at the construction industry in a wider context, architects as a professional body bring holistic design skills and and problem-solving that facilitate management across professional boundaries. This may be in the context of the demand side as the expert client adviser who assists the whole team or on the supply side as contributor to the design and construction process. In either situation the role of the architect as design manager remains an important one.

Whatever changes take place, in order to contribute effectively you will need to refresh your skills at some point or points in your professional career. The skills and knowledge you have acquired in Part 3 will provide a firm foundation for the inevitable changes that will occur in your future professional life.

NOTES

Chapter 1   Preparing for Part 3

1 Recognised Part 1 and Part 2 courses delivered by schools of architecture are validated by the RIBA and prescribed by the ARB. The roles of both organisations in maintaining the standards of architectural education are dealt with later. Strictly speaking, we should refer to courses as 'Part 1 equivalent' and 'Part 2 equivalent'.

2 Murdoch, J. and Hughes, W. (2005) *Construction Contracts: Law and Management* (3rd edn), London: Taylor and Francis.

3 For a good overview of the construction industry and the roles of the professions see Murdoch, J. and Hughes, W. (2005) London: Spon Press, chapters 1–3.

4 ARB website 2014 www.arb.org.uk

5 ARB website 2014 www.arb.org.uk

6 The ARB's statutory predecessor, ARCUK (the Architects' Registration Council of the United Kingdom), had responsibility for the EU Directive from the period 1985 to 1997.

7 The Privy Council formerly advised the Crown on government policy, a role now taken by the Cabinet. Its functions are mainly formal but it has limited statutory powers. One of these is to make Orders of Council, which mainly relate to the regulation of certain professions and professional bodies. (See note 12 below.)

8 The Architects Act 1997.

9 ARCUK was set up by statute and derived its powers from the Architects Acts of 1931–38.

10 RIBA Vision, July 2005 (available at www.architecture.com).

11 A Royal Charter is the way in which the Crown grants certain rights or privileges. In return for these privileges there is a certain measure of regulation (the Byelaws). Therefore the RIBA grew out of a professional membership organisation and was 'legitimised' by its Royal Charter. In addition to the 1837 Charter, Supplementary Charters were granted in 1887, 1909, 1925 and 1971. Full details of the Charter and Byelaws are available on the RIBA website.

12 RIBA website 2014 www.architecture.com

13 RIBA website 2014 www.architecture.com

14 As part of Mrs Thatcher's Conservative administration's review of regulation Sir George Young (one of her ministers) commissioned a report into the operation of ARCUK and the statutory registration and regulation of architects, which was perceived as 'seriously out of date'. The work was carried out by David Warne, who produced a report: 'The Review of Architects (Registration) Acts 1931–1969'. The report recommended the abolition of registration and ARCUK. On receiving the

report Sir George Young said: 'Statutory registration of architects has brought no lasting benefit to the public, to consumers nor to the profession itself' and 'that there is no reason only architects uniquely amongst construction professionals should be regulated by statute.' In the event the profession argued successfully that statutory regulation would safeguard the consumer and professional standards and the result was a streamlined regulator, the ARB. (*Architects Journal*, vol. 197, 10 February 1993, p. 6.)

15 'quango' is an acronym for 'quasi-autonomous non-governmental organisation'. There are hundreds of quangos which serve as small executive bodies set up for a particular purpose. They are broadly autonomous but rely upon government departments for their funding. Other quangos include English Heritage and the Design Council. One quango was less fortunate than the ARB in the government review: CABE – the Council for Architecture and the Built Environment. At one point it was due to be abolished completely but it has now become part of the Design Council.

16 This term includes the RIBA North-West Region, which delivers the Part 3 examination for Manchester and the two Liverpool schools. APEAS is the examining body for the six Scottish schools.

17 Since 1997 only one case has been appealed and the appeal was unsuccessful.

18 'Guidance on the RIBA Disciplinary Process and Procedures' RIBA Practice Department. The Guidance is issued for both complainants and RIBA members. The relevant basis for making an allegation is Byelaw 4.1 or 4.2 which also includes '...that a member has: contravened their election declaration' as well as the two other points referred to above.

19 Social theorists and commentators may also suggest that this is evidence of the professions 'closing ranks' in order to protect the reputation of professional institutions by ensuring consistency to meet their own objectives and sustain the 'status quo' and the respect of professions generally.

20 The judgement relates to the case of Professor Sir Roy Meadows, a specialist medical expert whose evidence at a trial was found to be flawed. He made an error by going beyond his medical knowledge and making a statistical judgement. The case was subsequently overturned. He was disciplined by the General Medical Council (GMC). He appealed and the judge reversed the GMC's ruling. In May 2006 Lord Goldsmith, the Attorney General, overruled the judge because there were public interest issues at stake, on the grounds that the professions should be responsible for disciplining their members and not the courts. In October 2006 Meadows won his appeal in the Court of Appeal (CA) based on the facts but the CA upheld the

principles set out by the Attorney General that trial experts did not have immunity and could be disciplined by their professional bodies.

21 University of Westminster *Part 3 Course Handbook 2005/2006*, p. 30. The skills referred to are based on standard Master's level 'SEEC' skills.

Chapter 2   Professional development

1 www.pedr.co.uk
2 The term 'office-based' refers to the RIBA Examination in Architecture for Office-Based Candidates managed for the RIBA by the Department of Architecture of Oxford Brookes University.
3 The ARB does not specify a format for recording your experience but schools of architecture universally use the PEDR.
4 ARB/RIBA Part 3 Criteria, *ARB Routes to Registration*, 2002, p. 23.

Chapter 3   Written examinations

1 Boris Johnson, *Daily Telegraph*, 12 May 2005.
2 It is not unheard of for candidates to run out of time during a two-day work-based examination. It does happen.
3 An exercise that you may find interesting is to look up what is written about 'Use Classes' in standard reference books and consider whether:

    a) the level of detail is appropriate to 'everyday' needs; and
    b) it is sufficiently comprehensive to be relied on.

4 Ostime, N. and Stanford, D. (2010) *Architect's Handbook of Practice Management*, London: RIBA Publications.
5 Lupton S, (2006) *Guide to SBC05*, London: RIBA Publishing
6 See Lupton S, (2006) *Guide to SBC05*, London: RIBA Publishing, p. 96–100. The costs associated with this claim will normally be decided by the quantity surveyor. Fortunately you only need to show you understand that it is an issue and that more information is needed.

Chapter 4   The case study

1   The requirements of the professional bodies should also be seen against the backdrop of a changing, sometimes innovative, construction industry which, influenced by the Latham and Egan Reports, is being driven towards achieving comparable projects at lower cost and within shorter timescales. These lower costs are derived largely by new contractual arrangements between contractors, subcontractors and suppliers that demand greater efficiency through teamwork, partnership and negotiation rather than more traditional, apparently stable contractual relationships. Coupled with this is the range in scale of both architectural practice and construction projects.

2   It is for these reasons that students need to have a basic but sound knowledge of 'traditional' forms of agreements for both professional services and construction contracts as well as those forms that they are familiar with in their limited office experience. Professional Part 3 examiners will probe that knowledge and understanding and will need to be satisfied that students understand them.

3   Management contracting in its various forms with differing levels of subcontractor design input tends to be used on these larger contracts. Partnership and Framework Agreements may be entered into by contractors and architects. The architect may have the status of the specialist subcontractor that happens to provide design services.

4   This is the sort of process that the office will go through to see where their responsibilities and the scope of the appointment differ from the SFA norm or what would be acceptable to professional indemnity insurers.

5   Printed in Daily Telegraph, 14th April 2014, sourced from Manchester Evening News.

6   A legal term meaning 'beyond the powers'. In contractual terms this means doing something that the contract does not give you the power to do. For example, deduction of liquidated damages in an Interim Certificate.

7   The Latham Report – 'Constructing the Team'. (1997). Latham divides projects into three simple stages: 'pre-project', 'project' and 'post-project'. The 'pre-project' stage is concerned with overall strategy possibly before a project exists; the 'project' phase covers the conventional RIBA Work Stages to completion; the 'post-project' stage covers post-completion issues and is intended to show a continuum of decision-making that affects the total life cycle of the building. Although 'Constructing the Team' was written some time ago, at the end of the 1990s economic recession, it has been very influential in determining procurement and design management practices

in the construction industry. Also, other influential initiatives, such as partnering and the use of Key Performance Indicators (KPIs) grew directly from the Latham Report.

8   The word 'novation' is derived from the phrase 'de novo' or 'new' and refers to the common practice of the client entering into two contracts. It applies to design and build contracts. The first contract is with the architect and the design team who are employed to develop the early work stages of the design through to obtaining town planning consents and possibly the detailed design phase. Post-tender, the second, *new* contract is formed between the client and design and build contractor with the architect and possibly the whole design team employed direct by the contractor for the production information and construction phases of the project.

9   Health and safety legislation is European-wide. Its recent origins are in European legislation, however each member state enacts the legislation differently and with different levels of thoroughness. For example, in the UK we have the CDM Regulations. The government 'enacted' the European Directive through a 'ready-made' piece of legislation that pre-dated the Directive by some years – the Health & Safety at Work Act 1973. The government department with responsibility for the legislation – the Health and Safety Executive, the CDM Regulations and procedures are particular to the UK.

10 Public sector projects above a certain value, including projects that receive a significant amount of public funding, must follow European Union procurement rules, the latest version of which were published in 2006. This applies to architectural consultancy services as well as to construction projects.

11 A checklist might include: parts of a bespoke appointment, the collateral warranty (if any), unusual town planning consent conditions, the invitation to tender letter, the letter of intent (if any), Architect's Instructions, Interim Certificates, claims for extension(s) of time, relevant contractual correspondence, the Practical Completion Certificate, etc.

Chapter 5   The oral examination

1   For an interesting social history and insight into professionalism in the 18th-century Navy see Rodgers, N. A. M. (1986) *The Wooden World*, London: Fontana.

2   An example of Master's level standards can be found in the SEEC level descriptors: www.seec.org.uk

3   The point here is that the Fire Officer is likely to be involved because it is a building covered by the Fire Precautions Act 1971. You cannot use a Building Notice in this instance: the Fire Officer needs to consult the plans. Only a full plans application will do.

4   Schon, D. A. (1983) *The Reflective Practitioner: How Professionals Think in Action*, London: Temple Smith.

APPENDICES
APPENDIX 1: THE PART 3 PROFESSIONAL CRITERIA 2010

The requirements for Part 3 are specific UK requirements for registration and the five Professional Criteria at Part 3 are not fully derived from the Mutual Recognition of Professional Qualifications Directive [2005/36/EC].

Interpretation of Requirements at Part 3

For Part 3 courses and assessments, the Graduate Attributes of the successful candidate are reflected within the introductory paragraphs. The Professional Criteria at Part 3 exist within the paragraphs titled and numbered 1–5. The numbered subsections are for explanation and guidance only and do not form part of the Professional Criteria at Part 3.

The terms 'knowledge', 'understanding', 'ability' and 'skills' are used in the Professional Criteria to indicate the nature of achievement required as the student progresses through qualifications at Parts 1, 2 and 3.

The Professional Criteria at Part 3

Candidates wishing to sit the Professional Practice Examination in Architecture (Part 3) are normally required to have successfully completed a recognised qualification at Part 1 and Part 2 level, or their equivalent recognised examinations. In addition, candidates are required to have completed the relevant professional practice experience before undertaking the examination.

Each candidate's experience of learning and development in professional practice will differ, depending upon the type of project, type and location of practice and management processes undertaken, and the preparation for the examination must therefore be approached in a structured way.

The candidate should manage the relationship between professional experience and academic study to provide coverage of the Professional Criteria, presenting a critically reflective body of work that complies with the requirements of the professional studies adviser or course provider. To meet the Professional Criteria, the candidate's experience should include evidence of commercial awareness, self-management, professional competence and integrity. A successful candidate should also be able to demonstrate authorship, knowledge, effective communications skills, and reasoning and understanding in relation to all issues within the Professional Criteria outlined below.

PC1   Professionalism

A successful candidate will demonstrate overall competence and the ability to behave with integrity, in the ethical and professional manner appropriate to the role of architect. The candidate will have the skills necessary to undertake effective communication and presentation, organisation, self-management and autonomous working. The candidate will have a clear understanding of the architect's obligation to society and the profession, and a sufficient awareness of the limits of their competence and professional experience to ensure they are unlikely to bring the profession into disrepute.

Demonstration of an understanding of the following will contribute to this criterion being met:

1.1   Professional ethics
1.2   The architect's obligation to society and the protection of the environment
1.3   Professional regulation, conduct and discipline
1.4   Institutional membership, benefits, obligations and codes of conduct
1.5   Attributes of integrity, impartiality, reliability and courtesy
1.6   Time management, recording, planning and review
1.7   Effective communication, presentation, confirmation and recording
1.8   Flexibility, adaptability and the principles of negotiation
1.9   Autonomous working and taking responsibility within a practice context
1.10 Continuing professional development

PC2   Clients, users and delivery of services

A successful candidate will be able to demonstrate understanding of the range of services offered by architects and delivering those services in a manner prioritising the interests of the client and other stakeholders. The candidate will have the skills necessary to provide a competent service, both singly and as part of a team, including understanding of client needs, appropriate communication, programming, coordination and competent delivery. This will be supported by knowledge of the briefing process, forms and terms of appointment, the means of professional remuneration, relevant legislation, and the execution of appropriate programmed and coordinated project tasks.

Demonstration of an understanding of the following will contribute to this criterion being met:

2.1 Types of clients, their priorities and the management of the relationship
2.2 Briefing, organising and the programming of services appropriate to appointment
2.3 Architects' contracts, terms of engagement, scope of services and relevant legislation
2.4 Obligations to stakeholders, warranties and third party rights
2.5 Communication, progress reporting and the provision of appropriate and timely advice
2.6 Budget and financial awareness and cost monitoring or control
2.7 Responsibility for coordination and integration of design team input
2.8 Invoicing, payment of fees and financial management
2.9 Intellectual property rights and copyright law
2.10 Duty of care, professional liability, negligence and professional indemnity insurance

PC3   Legal framework and processes

A successful candidate will be able to demonstrate understanding of the legal context within which an architect must operate, and the processes undertaken to ensure compliance with legal requirements or standards. The candidate will have the skills necessary to positively interact with statutory and private bodies or individuals, and competently deliver projects within diverse legislative frameworks. This will be supported by knowledge of the relevant law, legislation, guidance and controls relevant to architectural design and construction.

Demonstration of an understanding of the following will contribute to this criterion being met:

3.1 The relevant UK legal systems, civil liabilities and the laws of contract and tort (delict in Scotland)
3.2 Planning and Conservation Acts, guidance and processes
3.3 Building regulations, approved documents and standards, guidance and processes
3.4 Land law, property law and rights of other proprietors
3.5 Terms within construction contracts implied by statute
3.6 Health and safety legislation and regulations
3.7 Statutory undertakers and authorities, their requirements and processes
3.8 Environmental and sustainability legislation
3.9 Historic buildings legislation
3.10 Accessibility and inclusion legislation

PC4 Practice and management

A successful candidate will be able to demonstrate understanding of the business priorities, required management processes and risks of running an architectural practice, and the relationship between the practice of architecture and the UK construction industry. The candidate will have the skills necessary to engage in business administration and ability to resource, plan, implement and record project tasks to achieve stated goals, either individually or within a team. This will be supported by knowledge of the nature of legal business entities, office systems, administration procedures and the relevant legislation.

Demonstration of an understanding of the following will contribute to this criterion being met:

4.1 The roles of architectural practice in the construction industry
4.2 External factors affecting construction and practice at national and international levels
4.3 Practice structures, legal status and business styles
4.4 Personnel management and employment-related legislation
4.5 Practice finance, business planning, funding and taxation
4.6 Marketing, fee calculation, bidding and negotiation
4.7 Resource management and job costing
4.8 Administration, quality management, QA systems, recording and review
4.9 Staff development, motivation, supervision and planning
4.10 Teamworking and leadership

PC5 Building procurement

A successful candidate will be able to demonstrate understanding of UK construction and contract law, construction procurement processes and the roles of built environment professionals. The candidate will have the skills necessary to plan project-related tasks, coordinate and engage in design team interaction, execute effective contract communication and resolve construction-related challenges and disputes. This will be supported by an understanding of contractual relationships, the obligations upon an architect acting as contract administrator, job-related administrative systems and the management of projects in the context of the candidate's professional experience.

Demonstration of an understanding of the following will contribute to this criterion being met:

5.1 Procurement methods, including for public and larger projects and relevant legislation
5.2 The effect of different procurement processes on programme, cost, risk and quality
5.3 Collaboration in construction and provisions for teamworking
5.4 Tendering methods, codes, procedures and project planning
5.5 Forms of contract and subcontract, design responsibility and third party rights
5.6 Application and use of contract documentation
5.7 Roles of design/construction team members and their interaction
5.8 Duties and powers of a lead consultant and contract administrator
5.9 Site processes, quality monitoring, progress recording, payment and completion
5.10 Claims, litigation and alternative dispute resolution methods

APPENDIX 2: USEFUL SOURCES AND LINKS

1. Approaching Part 3

www.architecture.com
www.arb.org.uk
www.buildingfutures.org.uk

RIBA

Standards of Conduct and Practice (2009) – essential reading.

Mission Statement and Byelaws – not essential reading but reference to them will give you an idea of how the professional bodies are regulated.

(All available on the RIBA website)

ARB

ARB Code of Conduct and Standards (2010) – essential reading.

Routes to Registration; Guidance on registering as an architect in the UK; Code of Conduct and Standards – essential reading.

The Architects Act 1997 – not essential reading but it gives you an idea of the purpose of the ARB.

Professional Conduct Committee hearings – the summaries of the hearings on the ARB website give an indication of how the ARB applies the Standards sanctions available in the Code.

(All available on the ARB website)

REFLECTIVE SKILLS

Schon, D. A. (1991) *The Reflective Practitioner: How Professionals Think in Action*, London: Temple Smith – this is not essential reading but many people quote Schon without reading him. It is based on research into the professions, includes

194

observations from architectural students and tutors and is one of the sources of the idea of reflection.

2. Professional development

www.pedr.co.uk
www.architecture.com
www.arb.org.uk

3. The case study

RIBA

Clients Guide to Appointing an Architect

Standard Form of Agreement

Plan of Work (2013)

Ostime, N. RIBA Job Book (9th edition).

Ostime, N. and Stanford, D. (2010) *Architect's Handbook of Practice Management*, London: RIBA Publications.

Lupton, S. *SBC 11*, London: RIBA Enterprises – Lupton is an acknowledged expert on standard forms of contract and has written a good series of books on the JCT forms. It is advisable to buy at least the text that covers the JCT form that you are using in your case study or the closest to the contract you are using.

Murdoch, J. and Hughes, W. *Construction Contracts*, 4th edition, Oxon: Spons Press – this book gives a very clear overview of the construction industry and how different types of procurement and contract may apply.

Speight, A. and Stone, G. (eds) *Architects Legal Handbook*, 9th edition, Oxford: Architectural Press – a good introduction to the main legal areas that affect architectural practice and a standard text for many years.

Brookhouse, S. (2013) Professional Studies in Architecture.

4. After Part 3

RIBA – CPD Guidelines (see RIBA website and Appendix 6)

Foxell, S. (ed) (2003) *The Professionals' Choice*, London: RIBA – an interesting and provocative series of articles and papers compiled by the joint CABE RIBA Building Futures group. It contains some good references for further reading.

5. Useful contacts

APSAA

APSAA is the organisation representing Professional Studies Advisors.

www.apsaa.org.uk

ARCHITECTS REGISTRATION BOARD (ARB)

Architects Registration Board
8 Weymouth Street
London
W1W 5BU

The Architects Registration Board (ARB) is the statutory regulatory body established to protect the consumer and safeguard the reputation of architects. The website is a useful source of information about the ARB and its functions.

Tel: 020 7580 5861
Email: info@arb.org.uk
Web: www.arb.org.uk
Contact: Emma Matthews; Elaine Stowell

CAREERS IN ARCHITECTURE WEBSITE

www.careersinarchitecture.net

PEDR WEBSITE

This is the website dedicated to professional development for architectural students. It is a very useful source of information for students in the workplace. By subscribing annually it allows you to record your professional experience in the workplace online in a standardised way to meet the requirements of Part 3.

www.pedr.co.uk

RIBA

Royal Institute of British Architects
66 Portland Place
London
W1B 1AD

The RIBA is the professional organisation for architects. The website is a good source of information about the RIBA and has useful links.

Tel: 020 7580 5533
Public Information Line: 0906 302 0400
Email: info@inst.riba.org
Web: www.architecture.com
Contact: Joanna Parry in the Education Department

APPENDIX 3: SCHOOLS OF ARCHITECTURE OFFERING PART 3 IN THE UK AND OTHER PROVIDERS

ARCEX

The Executive Suites
Weavers Court Business Park
Linfield Road
Belfast BT12 5GH

Email: info@arcex.co.uk
Web: www.arcex.co.uk

ARCHITECTS' PROFESSIONAL EXAMINATIONS AUTHORITY IN SCOTLAND (APEAS) LTD

Room 21
Grangemouth Enterprise Centre
Falkirk Road
Grangemouth FK3 8XS

Tel: 01324 484652
Email: info@apeas.org.uk
Web: www.apeas.org.uk

ARCHITECTURAL ASSOCIATION

School of Architecture
34–36 Bedford Square
London WC1B 3ES

Tel: 020 7887 4000
Email: info@aaschool.ac.uk
Web: www.aaschool.ac.uk

BIRMINGHAM CITY UNIVERSITY

Birmingham School of Architecture
Birmingham Institute of Art and Design
Costa Green
Corporation Green
Birmingham B4 7DX

Tel: 0121 331 5130
Email: info@uce.ac.uk
Web: www.birminghamschoolofarchitecture.co.uk

BIRMINGHAM CITY UNIVERSITY

Faculty of the Built Environment
Perry Barr
Birmingham B42 2SU

Tel: 0121 331 5100
Web: www.scu.ac.uk

DE MONTFORT UNIVERSITY

The Leicester School of Architecture
Faculty of Art and Design
The Gateway
Leicester LE1 9BH

Tel: 0116 257 7555
Email: artanddesign@dmu.ac.uk
Web: www.dmu.ac.uk

EDINBURGH COLLEGE OF ART

School of Architecture
Lauriston Place
Edinburgh EH3 9DF

Tel: 0131 221 6000
Email: registry@eca.ac.uk
Web: www.eca.ac.uk

EDINBURGH SCHOOL OF ARCHITECTURE

c/o The University of Edinburgh
Department of Architecture
20 Chambers Street
Edinburgh EH1 1JZ

Tel: 0131 650 2342
Email: architecture@ed.ac.uk
Web: www.architecture.ed.ac.uk

KINGSTON UNIVERSITY

School of Architecture and Landscape
Knights Park
Kingston upon Thames
Surrey KT1 2QJ

Tel: 020 8547 7194
Web: www.kingston.ac.uk

LEEDS METROPOLITAN UNIVERSITY

School of the Built Environment
Faculty of Health and Environment
Brunswick Building
Leeds LS2 8BU

Tel: 0113 283 3217
Email: beenquiries@leedsmet.ac.uk
Web: www.lmu.ac.uk

LIVERPOOL JOHN MOORES UNIVERSITY

Liverpool School of Art and Design
Centre for Architecture
Kingsway House
Hatton Garden
Liverpool L3 2AJ
(administered by RIBA North West)

Tel: 0151 231 3704
Email: recruitment@livjm.ac.uk
Web: www.livjm.ac.uk

LONDON METROPOLITAN UNIVERSITY

Department of Architecture and Spatial
Design
Spring House
40–44 Holloway Road
London N7 8JL

Tel: 020 7133 2199
Web: www.asd.londonmet.ac.uk

LONDON SOUTH BANK UNIVERSITY

Faculty of Engineering, Science and Built
Environment
103 Borough Road
London SE1 0AA

Tel: 020 7815 7102
Email: rooneymj@lsbu.ac.uk
Web: www.lsbu.ac.uk

OXFORD BROOKES UNIVERSITY

School of Architecture
School of the Built Environment
Gipsy Lane Campus
Headington
Oxford OX3 0BP

Tel: 01865 483 200
Email: arch@brookes.ac.uk
Web: www.brookes.ac.uk

RIBA NORTH WEST REGION LIVERPOOL

Unit 101 The Tea Factory
82 Wood Street
Liverpool L1 4DQ

Tel: 0151 703 0107
Email: riba.northwest@inst.riba.org

THE ROBERT GORDON UNIVERSITY

The Scott Sutherland School of Architecture
& Built Environment
Robert Gordon University
Garthdee Road
Aberdeen AB10 7QB
(administered by APEAS)

Tel: 01224 263700
Email: sss@rgu.ac.uk
Web: www.rgu.ac.uk

THE QUEEN'S UNIVERSITY OF BELFAST

School of Architecture
2 Lennoxvale
Belfast BT9 5BY

Tel: 028 9027 4198
Email: architecture@qub.ac.uk
Web: www.qub.ac.uk

UNIVERSITY COLLEGE LONDON

The Bartlett School of Architecture
Wates House
22 Gordon Street
London WC1H 0QB

Tel: 020 7679 7504
Email: architecture@ucl.ac.uk
Web: www.bartlett.ucl.ac.uk

UNIVERSITY OF BATH

Department of Architecture and Civil
Engineering
Bath BA2 7AY
Tel: 01225 826654
Email: D.Griffiths@bath.ac.uk
Web: www.bath.ac.uk

UNIVERSITY OF BRIGHTON

School of Architecture and Design
Mithras House
Lewes Road
Brighton BN2 4AT

Tel: 01273 600 900
Web: www.bton.ac.uk

UNIVERSITY OF CAMBRIDGE

Department of Architecture
1 Scroope Terrace
Cambridge CB2 1PX

Tel: 01223 332 950
Email: arct-info@lists.cam.ac.uk
Web: www.arct.cam.ac.uk

UNIVERSITY OF CARDIFF

The Welsh School of Architecture
Bute Building
King Edward VII Avenue
Cardiff CF10 3NB

Tel: 029 2087 4430
Email: lupton@cardiff.ac.uk
Web: www.cf.ac.uk

UNIVERSITY OF DUNDEE

Faculty of Duncan Jordanstone College
School of Architecture
13 Perth Road
Dundee DD1 4HT
(administered by APEAS)

Tel: 01382 345 315
Email: school@architecture.dundee.ac.uk
Web: www.architecture.dundee.ac.uk

UNIVERSITY OF EDINBURGH

Department of Architecture
20 Chambers Street
Edinburgh EH1 1JZ
(administered by APEAS)

Tel: 0131 650 2342
Email: architecture@ed.ac.uk
Web: www.caad.ed.ac.uk

UNIVERSITY OF GLASGOW

The Mackintosh School
Department of Architecture
The Glasgow School of Art
167 Renfrew Street
Glasgow G3 6RQ
(administered by APEAS)

Tel: 0141 353 4500
Email: architecture@gsa.ac.uk
Web: www.gsa.ac.uk

UNIVERSITY OF GREENWICH

School of Architecture and Construction
Mansion Site
Bexley Road
Eltham SE9 2UG

Tel: 020 8331 9108
Email: courseinfo@gre.ac.uk
Web: www.gre.ac.uk

UNIVERSITY OF HUDDERSFIELD

Department of Architecture
The School of Design Technology
Queensgate
Huddersfield HD1 3DH

Tel: 01484 472 281
Email: architecture@hud.ac.uk
Web: www.des-tech.hud.ac.uk

UNIVERSITY OF LINCOLN

The Lincoln School of Architecture
Brayford Pool
Lincoln LN6 7TS

Tel: 01522 837 137
Web: www.lincoln.ac.uk

UNIVERSITY OF LIVERPOOL

Liverpool School of Architecture and
Building Engineering
Leverhulme Building
Abercromby Square
Liverpool L69 3BX
(administered by RIBA North West)

Tel: 0151 794 2606
Email: archweb@liv.ac.uk
Web: www.liv.ac.uk

UNIVERSITY OF MANCHESTER AND MANCHESTER METROPOLITAN UNIVERSITY

The Manchester School of Architecture
Chatham Building
Cavendish Street
Manchester M15 6BR
(administered by RIBA North West)

Tel: 0161 275 6950
Email: msa@mmu.ac.uk
Web: www.msa.mmu.ac.uk

UNIVERSITY OF NEWCASTLE UPON TYNE

School of Architecture, Planning and
Landscape
Newcastle upon Tyne NE1 7RU

Tel: 0191 222 5831
Web: www.apl.ncl.ac.uk

UNIVERSITY OF NOTTINGHAM

The Nottingham Institute of Architecture
University Park
Nottingham NG7 2RD

Tel: 0115 951 3174
Email: shaun.smith@nottingham.ac.uk
Web: www.nottingham.ac.uk

UNIVERSITY OF PORTSMOUTH

School of Architecture
Portland Building
Portland Street
Portsmouth PO1 3AH

Tel: 023 9284 8484
Email: architectureadmissions@port.ac.uk
Web: www.port.ac.uk

UNIVERSITY OF STRATHCLYDE

Department of Architecture
131 Rotten Row
Glasgow G4 0NG
(administered by APEAS)

Tel: 0141 458 3023
Email: architecture@strath.ac.uk
Web: www.strath.ac.uk

UNIVERSITY OF THE WEST OF ENGLAND

Faculty of the Built Environment
Frenchay Campus
Coldharbour Lane
Bristol BS16 1QY

Tel: 0117 328 3000
Email: wendy.colvin@uwe.ac.uk
Web: www.built-environment.uwe.ac.uk

UNIVERSITY OF WESTMINSTER

School of Architecture and the Built
Environment
Faculty of the Environment
35 Marylebone Road
London NW1 5LS

Tel: 020 7911 5000
Email: mrdmark@wmin.ac.uk
Web: www.wmin.ac.uk

APPENDIX 4: APSAA
Association of Professional Studies Advisors in Architecture

MENTOR'S GUIDE

What is a mentor? One dictionary definition is: a trusted teacher or advisor; a more senior colleague appointed to help and advise a junior employee. In Greek, Mentor is the name of the character in Homer's poems, who was advisor to Telemachus, Odysseus's son.

Professional experience forms a critical part of a candidate's education and training to become an architect. The employment mentor's role in advising, supporting and reviewing the candidate's professional experience is fundamental if the candidate is to benefit from their professional experience.

Professional Studies Advisor (PSA)

If a student or a mentor wishes to discuss any aspect of their role they should contact the student's Professional Studies Advisor (PSA). The PSA is usually a member of staff at a school of architecture who is responsible for providing guidance to students during their practical training and helping students prepare for the Part 3 Examination.

Employment mentor

Some students start their practical training at the age of 18: others will need a mentor's help even though they're 50. Similarly employment mentors vary in age and experience. A mentor should be a registered architect nominated by the office to ensure that the student is obtaining experience of design, construction, office procedures and contractual issues. If a student is doing their experience in the office of an engineer or another member of the design team the mentor should be a member of the professional body relevant to their discipline.

A good mentor is a competent, knowledgeable practitioner, who is approachable and reliable. They should also be a good listener and communicator. A mentor should regularly meet with their student and sign the candidate's record of experience at three-monthly intervals. They should offer day-to-day support and make the student aware of 'best practice'.

The key responsibilities of an Employment Mentor can be summarised as follows:

> To establish and maintain an organisational framework within the office which ensures that the candidate has access to high-quality professional experience and that they are supervised while in the office and out on site.
> To oversee the educational and professional development of the candidate, supervising his/her daily work, and reviewing the candidate's performance at quarterly intervals using a Record of Experience such as the RIBA PEDR or other form of record keeping.
> To ensure that students have sufficient time off at both post Part 1 and post Part 2 stages to broaden the breadth of their professional experience and to attend appropriate activities (e.g. university courses, CPD events and Part 3 seminars, etc.).
> To ensure that a candidate is not routinely given tasks that are of little or no educational or developmental value and that they are not unduly challenged by a task inappropriate to his/her current level of experience.
> To ensure that the student has a contract of employment and a detailed job description setting out the hours of work and the time allotted for professional study and that the student is inducted into appropriate health and safety legislation, procedures and practices in the office and on site.

The challenge for Employment Mentors is to balance the input into the professional development of their candidate. Mentors should not 'spoon feed' their mentee but encourage the student to explore, examine, question and reflect on a range of issues in architectural practice.

Things Employment Mentors can do to help students gain the most from their professional experience

> At the start of each quarter it is a good idea for the mentor and student to meet to review the previous quarter of experience and to set out work objectives and learning opportunities. Such meetings allow mentor and student to assess honestly and impartially the value of the experience.

> The written comments made by the mentor in the record sheets are important to the student's development. However, they are also important to professional Part 3 examiners. They allow examiners to see how the student has developed in practice. Mentors should make their written comments legible.
> Any comments made should accurately reflect discussions with the student. Any notable achievements should be commented on in the record sheets. However, comments should not 'shy away' from recording any areas of weakness. Comments can provide the stimulus for real improvement and form part of the work objectives for future periods of professional experience.

Employment Mentors are free to comment on the content of PEDR record sheets and may wish to address the following questions:

> Has the student signed and dated the sheets in the appropriate place?
> Are the contents of the record sheets clear and accurate?
> Is there too little or too much detail in the content of the record sheets?
> Is the student being sufficiently self-evaluative with regard to his/her experience?
> Do the record sheets contain details that clearly identify different jobs? (e.g. project title, contract value or budget costs, job stage and type of contract). Is there a sufficient number of illustrations/drawings to clarify the type of work and experience that is being undertaken? Are the illustrations/drawings clear and well presented?

The student

A student's responsibilities can be summarised as follows:

> To contribute fully to the work of the office including working co-operatively with others to achieve work completion to schedule.
> To comply with the ARB Standards of Professional Conduct and Practice and the Code of Professional Conduct as set out by RIBA and Health And Safety legislation, regulations, procedures and practices at all times.
> To study and comply with the office policy on intellectual property and the digital copying of work done in the office.
> To take full responsibility for his/her own work subject to supervision by the mentor and for their own learning so that by the end of their period of professional experience they are in a position to take on the responsibilities of a registered architect.
> To complete their Record of Experience on a three-monthly basis in a fair, open and accurate way, agreeing with their mentor in advance any office materials that can be included in the Record.

Ultimate responsibility for professional experience rests with the student. Students are strongly advised to monitor the range of experience across the various work stages at regular intervals. It is good practice for students to summarise the percentage of experience in each work stage.

Where gaps are revealed in work stages the mentor should, where practical, take every reasonable step to ensure that the student has opportunities to broaden their experience.

As with Employment Mentors, the responsibilities of students are set out clearly on the PEDR website (see PEDR website – Duties and Responsibilities of the Employer and Duties and Responsibilities of the Student).

PAYMENT FOR WORK

In the current economic climate some students are being offered unpaid work experience. The RIBA has published guidelines on recommended minimum conditions of employment for students.

APPENDIX 5

The table below shows how the new Plan of Work maps to the old RIBA Plan of Work 2007

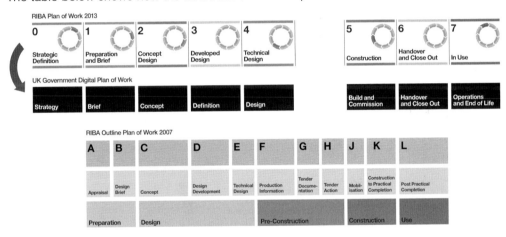

RIBA

The **RIBA Plan of Work 2013** organises the process of briefing, designing, constructing, maintaining, operating and using building projects into a number of key stages. The content of stages may vary or overlap to suit specific project requirements.

RIBA Plan of Work 2013

Stages ▶

Tasks ▼	**0** **Strategic Definition**	**1** **Preparation and Brief**	**2** **Concept Design**	**3** **Developed Design**
Core Objectives	Identify client's **Business Case** and **Strategic Brief** and other core project requirements.	Develop **Project Objectives**, including **Quality Objectives** and **Project Outcomes**, **Sustainability Aspirations**, **Project Budget**, other parameters or constraints and develop **Initial Project Brief**. Undertake **Feasibility Studies** and review of **Site Information**.	Prepare **Concept Design**, including outline proposals for structural design, building services systems, outline specifications and preliminary **Cost Information** along with relevant **Project Strategies** in accordance with **Design Programme**. Agree alterations to brief and issue **Final Project Brief**.	Prepare **Developed Design**, including coordinated and updated proposals for structural design, building services systems, outline specifications, **Cost Information** and **Project Strategies** in accordance with **Design Programme**.
Procurement *Variable task bar	Initial considerations for assembling the project team.	Prepare **Project Roles Table** and **Contractual Tree** and continue assembling the project team.	←- The procurement strategy does not fundamentally alter the progression of the design or the level of detail prepared at	a given stage. However, **Information Exchanges** will vary depending on the selected procurement route and **Building Contract**. A bespoke **RIBA Plan of Work**
Programme *Variable task bar	Establish **Project Programme**.	Review **Project Programme**.	Review **Project Programme**.	←- The procurement route may dictate the **Project Programme** and result in certain stages overlapping
(Town) Planning *Variable task bar	Pre-application discussions.	Pre-application discussions.	←- Planning applications are typically made using the Stage 3 output.	A bespoke **RIBA Plan of Work 2013** will identify when the
Suggested Key Support Tasks	Review **Feedback** from previous projects.	Prepare **Handover Strategy** and **Risk Assessments**. Agree **Schedule of Services**, **Design Responsibility Matrix** and **Information Exchanges** and prepare **Project Execution Plan** including **Technology** and **Communication Strategies** and consideration of **Common Standards** to be used.	Prepare **Sustainability Strategy, Maintenance and Operational Strategy** and review **Handover Strategy** and **Risk Assessments**. Undertake third party consultations as required and any **Research and Development** aspects. Review and update **Project Execution Plan**. Consider **Construction Strategy**, including offsite fabrication, and develop **Health and Safety Strategy**.	Review and update **Sustainability, Maintenance and Operational** and **Handover Strategies** and **Risk Assessments**. Undertake third party consultations as required and conclude **Research and Development** aspects. Review and update **Project Execution Plan**, including **Change Control Procedures**. Review and update **Construction** and **Health and Safety Strategies**.
Sustainability Checkpoints	Sustainability Checkpoint — 0	Sustainability Checkpoint — 1	Sustainability Checkpoint — 2	Sustainability Checkpoint — 3
Information Exchanges (at stage completion)	Strategic Brief.	Initial Project Brief.	**Concept Design** including outline structural and building services design, associated **Project Strategies**, preliminary **Cost Information** and **Final Project Brief**.	**Developed Design**, including the coordinated architectural, structural and building services design and updated **Cost Information**.
UK Government Information Exchanges	Not required.	Required.	Required.	Required.

*Variable task bar – in creating a bespoke project or practice specific RIBA Plan of Work 2013 via www.ribaplanofwork.com a specific bar is selected from a number of options.

The **RIBA Plan of Work 2013** should be used solely as guidance for the preparation of detailed professional services contracts and building contracts.

www.ribaplanofwork.com

4 Technical Design	5 Construction	6 Handover and Close Out	7 In Use
Prepare **Technical Design** in accordance with **Design Responsibility Matrix** and **Project Strategies** to include all architectural, structural and building services information, specialist subcontractor design and specifications, in accordance with **Design Programme**.	Offsite manufacturing and onsite **Construction** in accordance with **Construction Programme** and resolution of **Design Queries** from site as they arise.	Handover of building and conclusion of **Building Contract**.	Undertake **In Use** services in accordance with **Schedule of Services**.
2013 will set out the specific tendering and procurement activities that will occur at each stage in relation to the chosen procurement route.	Administration of **Building Contract**, including regular site inspections and review of progress.	Conclude administration of **Building Contract**.	
or being undertaken concurrently. A bespoke **RIBA Plan of Work 2013** will clarify the stage overlaps.	The **Project Programme** will set out the specific stage dates and detailed programme durations.		
planning application is to be made.			
Review and update **Sustainability, Maintenance and Operational** and **Handover Strategies** and **Risk Assessments**. Prepare and submit Building Regulations submission and any other third party submissions requiring consent. Review and update **Project Execution Plan**. Review **Construction Strategy**, including sequencing, and update **Health and Safety Strategy**.	Review and update **Sustainability Strategy** and implement **Handover Strategy**, including agreement of information required for commissioning, training, handover, asset management, future monitoring and ongoing compilation of '**As-constructed' Information**. Update **Construction** and **Health and Safety Strategies**.	Carry out activities listed in **Handover Strategy** including **Feedback** for use during the future life of the building or on future projects. Updating of **Project Information** as required.	Conclude activities listed in **Handover Strategy** including **Post-occupancy Evaluation**, review of **Project Performance, Project Outcomes** and **Research and Development** aspects. Updating of **Project Information**, as required, in response to ongoing client **Feedback** until the end of the building's life.
Sustainability Checkpoint — 4	Sustainability Checkpoint — 5	Sustainability Checkpoint — 6	Sustainability Checkpoint — 7
Completed **Technical Design** of the project.	'**As-constructed' Information**.	Updated '**As-constructed' Information**.	'**As-constructed' Information** updated in response to ongoing client **Feedback** and maintenance or operational developments.
Not required.	Not required.	Required.	As required.

© RIBA

APPENDIX 6

RIBA ⊞

RIBA CPD Core Curriculum Study Guide

1. Being safe health and safety

Possible topics

*Pertinent construction legislation and building regulations
*CDM (or similar outside the UK), particularly designers' responsibilities
*Workplace health and safety
*Employers' responsibilities
*Risk assessment
*Fire safety legislation
*CSCS card procurement

2. Climate: sustainable architecture

Possible topics

A. Briefing

*Knowledge of climate change and climate change science and impact of both mitigation and adaptation
*KPI's and which ones should be used
*Communicating the importance of low carbon design
*Understanding stakeholders, clients, planning and legislative authorities
*Defining the brief whilst balancing sustainability targets
*Understanding and prioritising energy efficiency in low carbon design
*Importance of sustainable design from inception to completion and handover including post-occupancy evaluation and feedback
*Understanding the impact of choices on traditional and old buildings

B. Design process

*Regulations, codes, guidance and standards (current and planned)
*Heat loss parameters and understanding the relationship between air tightness, insulation, glazing, heat loss and solar gain.
*Building services and renewable energy systems
*Building energy performance/metering and monitoring
*Understanding the energy assessment process
*Material selection, embedded energy, recycling and minimising waste
*Understanding energy and u-value calculations
*When to use passive or mechanical ventilation
*Whole life carbon footprinting
*Resource energy efficiency, materials, water, energy and behaviour
*Understanding sustainable benchmarking tools and assessment methods: BREEAM, SAP, PHPP, Code for Sustainable Homes, EARM

3. External management: clients, users and delivery of services

Possible topics

*Architects' contracts (eg, as lead or sub consultant), terms of engagement, scope of services, clear letters of appointment, relevant legislation

66 Portland Place
London W1B 1AD UK
Tel +44 (0)20 7580 5533
Fax +44 (0)20 7255 1541
info@inst.riba.org
www.architecture.com

Public Information line
0906 302 0400*

Registered Charity Number 210 566
VAT Registration Number 232 351 891
*call charged at 50p per minute

RIBA ♔

*Intellectual property rights, copyright law
*Duty of care, professional liability, negligence and professional indemnity, including insurance
*Client relationship management
*Briefing/getting the brief right/context of the brief
*Adding value through design and services
*Obligations to stakeholders, warranties and third party rights
*Communication, progress reporting and appropriate and timely advice
*Cost monitoring and control and financial management
*Programming of services appropriate to appointment
*Coordination + integration of design team input

4. Internal management: professionalism, practice, business + management

Possible topics

*Architect's obligation to society and the protection of the environment
*Practice structures, legal status and business styles
*Time management, recording, planning and review
*Effective communication, presentation, pitching, confirmation and recording
*Staff management and development
*Practice finance, business planning, funding and taxation
*Marketing and promoting the practice
*Fee calculation, negotiation, bidding
*Administration, quality management, QA systems, recording and review
*Team working and leadership
*Resource management, job costing and cash flow
*Risk management
*Project management
*Current RIBA and ARB codes of conduct and discipline, including professional ethics

5. Compliance: legal, regulatory and statutory frameworks and processes

Possible topics

*The relevant UK (or overseas if you work elsewhere) legal systems and processes, civil liabilities and the laws of contract and tort (delict)
*Planning, Listed Buildings and Conservation Areas Acts, guidance and processes (see also section 9)
*Building regulations, EU regulations, ISOs, approved documents and standards, guidance and processes, such as The Equality Act 2010, Health and Safety, fire safety, environmental
*Land law, property law, The Party Wall Act, and rights of other proprietors
*Terms within construction contracts implied by statute
*Statutory undertakers and authorities, their requirements and processes
*Employment-related legislation and policies
*Environmental and sustainability legislation (see also section 2)
*Accessibility, inclusion, and diversity legislation (see also section 10)
*Advisory design review systems
*Health and safety/CDM legislation and regulations (see also section 1)

6. Procurement and contracts

RIBA ⸙

Possible topics

*Procurement methods, including for public and larger projects and relevant legislation
*Tendering methods, codes, procedures and project planning
*Forms of contract and sub-contract, design responsibility and third-party rights
*Claims, litigation and alternative dispute resolution methods
*The effect of different procurement routes on programme, cost, risk, quality
*Collaboration and briefing in construction and provisions for team working
*Application and use of contract documentation
*Duties and powers of a lead consultant and contract administrator
*Site processes, quality monitoring, progress recording, payment and completion
*Project Management (as a qualified person)

7. Designing and building it: design, construction, technology and engineering

Possible topics

*Architectural design
*BIM, CAD, modelling, mapping and visualisation.
*Design for accessibility
*Technical innovations
*Specification writing and choosing materials
*Production information
*Alternative structural, construction and material systems
*Optimum physical, thermal and acoustic environments
*Systems for environmental comfort within the relevant precepts of sustainable design
*Strategies for building services and the integration within a design project

8. Where people live: communities, urban + rural design and the planning process

Possible topics

*The theories and objectives of urban design and the qualities of successful places
*The influence of design and development on places, communities, non urban areas and cities
*The needs and aspirations of communities, and space and building users
*The ways in which spaces and places fit into their local context
*The role played by design within the larger community context
*Understanding briefing, engagement, empowerment, cohesion and leadership and their impact on creating successful communities
*Understanding the relation between design, buildings, green spaces, gathering places, facilities, energy, carbon reduction, highways, servicing, safety and security and people

9. Context: the historic environment and its setting

Possible topics

RIBA 🏛

*Legislation and published governmental and other guidance relevant to historic
assets (buildings, areas, monuments, gardens and parks, whether designated yet or not)
and their settings, eg, Icomos
*Planning and Conservation Acts, guidance and processes
*Cultural significance
*Historical significance
*Architectural significance
*Settings
*Aesthetic qualities and values
* Investigation, materials, technology and the building environment
*Social, environmental and financial issues
*Implementation and management of conservation works
*Special considerations in the application of approved documents (including building
regulations, The Equality Act, environmental, fire safety)
*The impact of archaeological sites known or suspected on building
*The impact of green design choices on traditional and old buildings

10. Access for all: universal/inclusive design

Possible topics

*The principles of universal or accessible design
*Planning and access
*Equality and diversity legislation, including The Equality Act 2010, and relevant
building and other regulations
*Access and inclusion in the workplace
*Understanding, writing and implementing access statements
*Relevant product specification
*Community consultation and engagement and working with user groups
*Special issues for fire, security and egress
*Principal guidance standards
*Different buildings and their uses and users
*Design detailing, eg, colour and contrast, acoustics
*Fixtures, fittings and equipment
*Refurbishment of listed buildings and access
*Management policies, procurement and brief writing
*Lifetime Homes and wheelchair housing

What is the Certificate of Professional Experience?

The Certificate of Professional Experience is an alternative online recording format to the standard Professional Experience and Development Record (PEDR), which may be used, with permission from a Part 3 course leader, by Part 3 candidates with substantial experience.

Applying to use the Certificate of Professional Experience

Part 3 candidates with substantial experience, who have reached a degree of responsibility in their offices which gives them supervisory functions, may apply to their Part 3 course leader/Professional Studies Advisor for permission to use the RIBA Certificate of Professional Experience in lieu of the standard PEDR, provided that the following condition is met:

> The candidate must have at least 6 years' experience, all of which must have met the RIBA's *practical experience eligibility criteria*, and must have been undertaken outside of full-time academic study* for Part 1 and Part 2.

*Candidates who have studied on a part-time course or office-based route may apply to their Part 3 course leader to use the Certificates to record their experience.

Candidates wishing to apply should provide their Part 3 course leader with the following information:

> A statement of the length of their experience.
> A description of the kind of work they are currently undertaking, with the character and size of projects.
> A statement from their employer about their work and the level of responsibility they hold.

Because a Certificate of Professional Experience is of limited value to Part 3 examiners in assessing the quality of experience, it must be accompanied by a report and supplementary evidence, giving the student's own appreciation of the value of each employment to date. The 6 years' worth of experience should all be covered, and as a guideline, the report is expected to be around 2000 words; however, course providers may stipulate their exact requirements and thus candidates should check the exact requirements with their course provider.

Candidates should note that course providers may also ask them to complete standard PEDR sheets covering their current experience from the start of the Part 3 course, until the documentary submission date; and therefore submit their experience in a combination of the two recording formats.

Course providers will provide further guidance on their specific requirements.

A separate Certificate must be submitted in respect of each employment in which the candidate has obtained professional experience.

Aspects to consider when choosing which recording format to use

Candidates considering requesting permission to use the Certificate of Professional Experience should review the following information before applying to their course provider:

> The Certificate of Professional Experience is designed for the retrospective recording of prior experience.
> As above, some Part 3 course providers will advise that the standard quarterly PEDR sheets should also be completed for the candidate's ongoing experience in the lead-up to the Part 3 examination phase, and both standard sheets and relevant Certificates submitted for assessment.
> Candidates are reminded that whichever recording format they choose, the evidence they produce will be submitted for assessment at the Part 3 examination. Candidates should therefore consider carefully which format would be better suited to presenting their experience and to take advice from their course leader.
> At the discretion of the course provider, candidates may be required to submit their Certificates for interim review prior to the date of the final documentary submission.

How to complete a Certificate of Professional Experience

To complete a Certificate of Professional Experience online your first step is to register on the PEDR website. Once you have registered and signed in, click on 'Your Certificates' under the 'Certificates of Professional Experience' menu item. Then click on 'New Certificate'. This will take you to the general information section of your selected sheet and the menu will expand to display links to the other sections.

The best way to complete your certificate, especially when starting a new record, is to fill in the details on each page and then click on 'Save and proceed to the next step'. This will take you through all the sections you need to complete. Most sections can be left blank and you can return to them at any time using the menu options on the left.

Viewing and printing draft copies of your record

Partial or completed record sheets can be viewed by clicking on the 'View Record' menu item. Draft copies can be viewed and printed at any time. They will appear in a pop-up window in printer-friendly format. Use the print button on your web browser to print the record.

Submitting a Certificate of Professional Experience

The Certificate of Professional Experience must be signed by an employer to confirm the candidate has undertaken the activities recorded overleaf whilst in their employment. A letter of support from the employer to accompany the Certificate would also assist the examiners.

A separate Certificate must be submitted in respect of each employment in which the candidate has obtained professional experience.

www.pedr.co.uk/sample/certificates

23.03.2014

INDEX